A CASEBOOK:
Applications
of the
Myers-Briggs
Type Indicator
in
Counseling

Judith A. Provost, Ed.D.

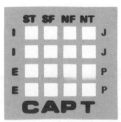

**CENTER FOR APPLICATIONS OF
PSYCHOLOGICAL TYPE, INC.**

Published by Center for Applications of Psychological Types, Inc.
P.O. Box 13807, Gainesville, Florida 32604

Copyright © 1984 by Judith A. Provost

Library of Congress Cataloging in Publication Data

Provost, Judith A., 1942—
    A casebook, applications of the Myers-Briggs Type Indicator in counseling.

    Bibliography: p.
    1. Myers-Briggs Type Indicator.   2. Counseling.
I. Title.
BF698.P722 1984 158'.3 84-21443
ISBN 0-935652-12-4

"For my family, who
taught me the
most about Type."

CONTENTS

PREFACE

For years I've been writing descriptions in my head of counseling interactions that involved the Myers-Briggs Type Indicator. As I drove to work or made the long drive to Gainesville during doctoral studies, those pages took shape in my mind. It was Mary McCaulley who encouraged me to get those vignettes down on paper. She reminded me in her gentle way of my Extraversion—that I might never get around to writing my ideas down, that ENFP's lived in danger (so to speak) of taking on many interesting projects and not following through. It is a tribute to Type development theory that I have accessed all my functions, not just my favorite Intuition, to write this casebook. One of the most useful aspects of the MBTI is its dynamic theory which allows for, and encourages, growth and change within basic personality Types. Understanding this theory has helped me to get organized and stick with this project.

When this casebook was first conceived, there was some question as to whether cases should come from the practices of a variety of practitioners or from a single practitioner. I decided to present cases only from my own practice to give the casebook continuity and flow and to demonstrate how one therapist, with a given MBTI Type and counseling orientation, worked with all 16 Types. I hope this book will spark others to share cases of counseling, organizational consultation, family therapy, to rethink Type, and to challenge my thinking! We can build upon the MBTI literature and thus all be richer for this shared knowledge. A second casebook is planned to include additional cases from other practitioners working in a variety of settings.

This casebook must claim the natural limitation of the author's perception of the world—that of an ENFP. My vocabulary, metaphors, or examples used to describe the world might sometimes be different from those of the other 15 Types. Of course, we are all limited by our own identities from seeing the world in the broadest sense. At best, we can be aware of some of our biases and assumptions and avoid talking in terms of absolutes. Later in the book the limitations of our own Types on our functioning as counselors/therapists will be explored.

A brief description of my clinical orientation and experience with the Myers-Briggs Type Indicator may be helpful to readers in weighing the usefulness of this casebook. My professional degrees include a master's degree in community mental health nursing from UCLA and the Ed.D. from the University of Florida's Department of Counselor Education. I have worked in psychiatric hospitals, community mental health centers, and college settings. I have a private practice in career counseling and psychotherapy and have done some consulting with organizations, utilizing the MBTI. My counseling orientation is primarily Gestalt Therapy, having trained with the Gestalt Institute of Florida. I employ a variety of other approaches as appropriate to the client and situation, such as Ellis' Rational Emotive Therapy and behavioral therapy.

I discovered the MBTI in my first college counseling position in 1974 and quickly became enthusiastic about its possibilities and hungry for more knowledge about the instrument. About that time CAPT (Center for Applications of Psychological Type) under Mary McCaulley's leadership and with Isabel Briggs Myers' support, was solidifying the professional use of the MBTI. In 1975, the first international conference on the MBTI was held in Gainesville, Florida. This conference and subsequent MBTI conferences and workshops have stimulated me to utilize the MBTI in my private and college practices and in conducting research. I have led BTMI workshops on national, regional, and local levels.

As Director of Personal Counseling in a four year liberal arts college, I have systematically administered the MBTI to all entering freshmen during orientation week. Because most students remain at the college for four years and live on campus, I have been able to "Type watch", observing first-hand the dynamic development of young Types over this four year period. Type development is at the core of MBTI theory and certainly at the core of counseling applications. These observations of young adults have given me an understanding of what is necessary for good Type development, as well as what will impede that development. In the living laboratory, which is a residential college, the effects of counseling interventions, of environmental factors, and of life events on the various Types can be observed. Socialization and relationship patterns of the 16 Types can also be followed. The stages and tasks identified in developmental psychology and the theory of Type development together form an extremely useful framework for counseling and therapy.

I am grateful to all the young people and clients who have enriched my life by allowing me to know them and to share in their discoveries. I treasure the many stimulating MBTI discussions with professional associates, especially with my APT and CAPT friends. A special thanks to Mary McCaulley, who enriches us all in our quest for fuller understanding of Type.

July, 1984
J.A.P.

Chapter I
PURPOSE OF THE CASEBOOK

This casebook is written for counselors and therapists who have already had an introduction to the Myers-Briggs Type Indicator. Readers should know their own Type and have a basic knowledge of the four preference scales, Carl Jung's theory of psychological Types, and the format and administration of the instrument. The casebook is not a subsitutute for reading the *MBTI Manual* or taking a workshop on the theory and use of the MBTI. There are excellent materials (distributed by CAPT) which are important background reading. I particularly recommend Isabel Briggs Myers' *Gifts Differing* (1980) for a sound and thorough, yet very readable, presentation of Type. Furthermore, it is assumed that readers who are practitioners will already have training in the use of psychometric instruments and a model for conducting counseling and therapy. Practitioners should already have some knowledge of therapies such as Gestalt and Rational Emotive Therapy; therefore these therapies will not be explained in any detail.

This casebook will demonstrate applications of the MBTI in individual counseling and psychotherapy with 18 cases representing various ages and presenting problems. Through these applications, readers can gain a deeper understanding of Type dynamics and Type development and, perhaps, a fresh angle from which to view Type. Selection of the specific cases for the book was made from my years of private and college counseling practice. Of the many possible cases, those were chosen which best exemplified the typical kinds of problems I encounter working with the 16 Types. There are more college-age clients (18-24) represented here, because these cases vividly demonstrate Type development problems and the relationship of Type to counseling interventions.

Because of these selection factors, these clients are above average intelligence and are, for the most part, in earlier stages of Type development than an older population. For example, a young ISTJ may demonstrate somewhat different characteristics than an older ISTJ because there has been less time to develop all the functions. The young ISTJ's may appear more narrow in interests and coping style. They may view the world in "black and white", arbitrary terms and may expect definitive answers from authority figures. Mature ISTJ's are likely to respect authority and tradition, yet be independent-minded. Although holding strong, even set, values and ways of dealing with the world, mature Types acknowledge other possibilities. However, all ISTJ's, young and old, male and female, will hold certain characteristics in common, such as their strong determination to do things in an efficient and practical manner. There is, of course, a wide range of individual differences within each of the 16 Types. Readers are thus cautioned that an immature Type may appear somewhat different from another, more mature individual of the same Type. More will be said about Type development in Chapter Two.

In addition to background theory in Chapter Two, Chapter Three, "Appropriate Use of the MBTI", discusses settings, appropriate clients, approaches to interpretation, and most importantly, ethics of use. The "18 Cases" are presented in Chapter Four. Finally, Chapter Five summarizes issues and dynamics in counseling with the MBTI.

Chapter II
TYPE DEVELOPMENT
AND COUNSELING

Understanding the process of psychological Type development is valuable in counseling clients. A model for normal Type development is summarized here. Again, I would refer readers to Myers' own words in *Gifts Differing* for a complete explanation. Some of my formulations are derived from conversations with other professionals using the MBTI in clinical settings.

The model for normal Type development postulates that everyone has four basic functions: two perception functions (Sensing, S, and Intuition, N) and two judgment functions (Thinking, T, and Feeling, F). Individuals differ in the order in which they develop these functions and in which functions they naturally prefer to use. In other words, for different Types there is a different developmental order and degree of use of these four functions. Developmental issues in counseling, therefore, are the following:

— Has the normal development order of the functions been interfered with? ...by what environmental or circumstantial factors? ...with what consequences?
— What has been the pattern of function development? ...implications for the client?
— How well can the client use the functions? Which are preferred? Which does the client have confidence in, and which does the client avoid? Are the consequences problematic?
— What can the counselor and client do to facilitate development of all four functions, but particularly of the natural functions? ...to develop a "balanced" personality, the ability to use the function appropriate to the situation and not to overuse or rely solely on one function?

The most preferred or favorite function is called the dominant. The second favorite is the auxiliary and serves as a back-up and balancing function to the dominant. If the dominant is a perception function (S or N), the auxiliary will be a judging function (T or F), or vice versa. Usually individuals develop their dominant function first and begin this development in childhood. Von Franz (1979), explaining Jung's theory, states that the dominant should be reflected in behavior by kindergarten age. Individuals direct most of their energy and attention to activities and interests which strengthen their favored function. Because this function comes naturally, individuals meet with success and obtain reinforcement for use of this function. Thus, they become "specialists" in that function. For example, in childhood those with dominant N might prefer games of imagination and make-believe, obtain much adult attention for their incredible stories, perhaps develop creative writing ability, get rewarded by teachers for creative work, and so on. These individuals with dominant N might pay little attention to S activities and interests such as mechanical or intricately detailed hobbies.

When individuals have developed their dominant functions, they typically turn their attention to exploration of their auxiliaries. Other kinds of activities or behaviors might be necessary to develop this back-up function. Auxiliary development usually begins in the young adult, but there is no specific time-table, other than the sequence itself. Readiness and environmental factors influence the timing of these developments.

Some MBTI experts favor explaining the dominant and auxiliary using the metaphor of handedness. If one is right-handed, the right hand is like the dominant function; use is natural, comfortable, more skillful. The left hand, or auxiliary, can be used but with much less grace. One would have to work much harder to do something with the same competence using the weaker hand. Having two hands, of course, provides balance needed for many activities. In the same way, dominant and auxiliary together provide balance. In several of the clinical cases, the lack of a developed auxiliary was associated with client imbalance and difficulty. For example, a dominant N without a balancing T or F auxiliary might plunge into a great number of projects without being able to evaluate whether the projects are appropriate or not.

The natural pattern of development, then, is from dominant (No. 1) to auxiliary (No. 2) to No. 3 (the function opposite No. 2) and to No. 4 (opposite the dominant, the least developed and least preferred function). The latter is sometimes referred to as the "shadow" because it is so difficult to access and is so primitive. The term "shadow" will not be used here to refer to the No. 4 function because of confusion with the earlier use of the term by Jung to describe the personal unconscious, undesirable aspects which the self represses. Also the term "shadow" can have a negative connotation, whereas the "least preferred" function is just that. If and when No. 4 (and No. 3) can be utilized in mature adulthood, the outcome is often positive, even exhilarating.

Von Franz, Jung, and others have speculated that most people may not truly begin to develop the fourth function until later in life, and at best it will always remain an elusive aspect of the personality. The path to transcending oneself, to obtaining heightened awareness and spirituality lies with accessing the less preferred functions. Most successful meditation approaches create ways to access the 4th function. But this is a topic fascinating enough to become a book in itself!

4

Readers may observe that so far we have only discussed two of the four MBTI scales having to do with the basic functions of perception (S-N) and judgment (T-F). The other two scales, the Extravert-Introvert (E-I) and Judgment-Perception (J-P), are attitudes, **not** functions. These attitudes indicate an individual's dominant and auxiliary and how these functions are used. The J-P scale reflects the preferred functional style for dealing with the **outer** world. People with a Judgment preference use a judgment function (T or F) to structure and organize their lives. People preferring Perception use a perception function (S or N) to discover and experience life spontaneously.

Extraverts' dominant function is the one they use with the **outer** world. Thus, an ENFJ:

— deals with the outer world with Feeling, a J function,
— and F is the dominant function,
— N is therefore the auxiliary function.

Introverts, on the other hand, deal with the outer world with their auxiliary, preserving their dominant for their internal world. Thus, an INFJ:

— deals with the outer world with the auxiliary F
— and N is the dominant, internalized function.

The simplest rule to remember how to identify dominant and auxiliary is:

1. J-P indicates the dominant for **Extraverts**
2. J-P indicates the auxiliary for **Introverts**

Thus, the importance of noting all four scales and their combined effect becomes apparent. Each of the 16 Types is a specific development map indicating the natural order of function development, the preferred and least preferred functions, and how they are used in the inner (self) and outer worlds.

To reinforce this explanation, each case in Chapter Four will have a notation to indicate the order of function development. For example, the notation for an ESTJ will look like this:

EXTRAVERTED THINKING
with Sensing
ESTJ

T
S
N
F

"Extraverted Thinking" means that thinking is the dominant function and is extraverted, or used in dealing with the outer world. "With sensing" means sensing is the auxiliary function and is introverted. The functions are listed in descending order from dominant No. 1, T, to No. 4, F.

"Introverted Thinking with sensing" means that the dominant function, thinking, is introverted and the auxiliary, sensing, is extraverted.

An interesting dynamic concerning Introverts' development of dominant and auxiliary should be noted at this point. An Introvert may develop the auxiliary more quickly or more thoroughly than the dominant in order to have a way of interacting with the world. Consequently, I often see Introverts with both No. 1 and No. 2 well-developed and Extraverts with just the dominant developed, since the latter are not forced to develop the back-up function to interact with their world.

Of course, life or environmental circumstances and age have a great deal to do with **what** and **how** we develop. Although each individual has natural preferences, the environment may shape which functions developed first and to what degree. For example, a child with a dominant F might first develop the auxiliary S or N if the home environment discouraged expression of Feeling.

These dynamics become important when working with clients, since interventions should utilize already existing coping mechanisms and strengths and encourage development of the other MBTI functions as well. Identifying strengths is particulary helpful in crisis situations. If a therapist is working with an ESTJ client, the therapist must first appeal to the client's sense of logic (T) and secondly give concrete examples (S) in structuring interventions. Clients who appear to rely too heavily or solely on one function, usually the dominant, can be helped to develop more balance through exercising one of the other functions as well. The counselor's goal, in the broadest sense, is to help clients develop all their functions so that they are capable of using the function appropriate to a given situation, capable of working in harmony with various aspects (functions) within themselves. Of course, there is a maturational factor here which prevents the therapist from being able to artificially move the client to a further state of development before the client is ready. For example, the counselor may identify the need to develop one of the judging functions, but the client may not be ready or willing to work toward that end. The client's goal for counseling may differ from the counselor's. The therapist, however, can offer opportunities and guidance to help the individual in developing the other functions. The process may be very gradual and continue long after therapy is terminated.

Another benefit of knowing clients' Type is anticipating potential areas of difficulty. From the model, counselors can draw a set of expectations (general parameters) about client behavior, coping style, and developmental tasks or problems. For example, the counselor could anticipate that a young INTP might have difficulty relating to peers. Here the dominant function is T and the least preferred, and most likely undeveloped, is F. He **might** appear Eccentric, reticent, puzzling, strongly individualistic, and possibly antisocial to his peers. Note the stress on "might". One cannot generalize about the level of development without interview data and ongoing observations. The MBTI reflects a dynamic, not static, theory of personality and as an instrument is thus more of a guide than a diagnosis, a process more than an outcome. Another INTP may utilize Intuition effectively to see the patterns in his relationships and find creative ways to interact with others and still preserve his individuality. The cases in Chapter Four will illustrate use of the Type developmental model for counseling.

In summary, this chapter has presented a model for personality development based on Type theory. The model suggests to counselors potential developmental difficulties, as well as strengths and weaknesses of the various Types. Each of the 16 Types is a dynamic map of an individual's development from the dominant function, to the auxiliary, to the third, and finally to the least preferred function. Environmental factors may interfere with this natural order. Everyone has the potential for developing and utilizing all four functions over a lifespan. Counselors can assist in this development. Clients' MBTI Type should be viewed in the broader context of their age, environment, and stage of personal growth. Type does not stand on its own but must be seen in this context because of its interactive, dynamic nature. Chapter III will expand on appropriate use of the MBTI.

Chapter III
USING THE MBTI

Professionals are encouraged to think through their use of the MBTI in terms of appropriate settings, purposes or outcomes desired, timing of administration, appropriate clients, and ethics. The MBTI should not be used indiscriminately or in "cookbook" fashion. Comments here serve as a supplement to, but not a substitute for, training in MBTI administration and interpretation.

Settings

The MBTI is valuable in many settings: in the private practice of counseling and psychotherapy, in consultation with organizations and businesses, and in educational institutions. The instrument can be administered to individuals or groups. In my primary setting, a college, most of my MBTI use has involved group administration. The MBTI is administered along with several academic placement tests to all freshmen during orientation week. Students who miss this group administration may take the MBTI by appointment any time during the year.

Example of Use in a College Setting

Before giving the standardized instructions for taking the Indicator, I introduce myself and the use of the MBTI. Freshmen are told that the results will be available to them within a few weeks to aid in adjustment to college, in choosing academic majors, and in career planning. They are told that when the results are back they will receive a memo with my phone number so they can make appointments for interpretation. They are told their results will be held until they are ready and interested in the interpretation. Confidentiality is stressed. Results are only available, and released, to the individual students themselves.

Many freshmen will come in for interpretation within a few months of receiving the memo, but many will wait until their sophomore year. To enhance the outreach, freshman advisors are also informed that MBTI results are available to their advisees. Thus, in student-advisor conversations about academic direction and adjustment, the advisor can suggest a meeting with me to explore these issues in light of MBTI results. It is up to the student to decide whether to share results with the advisor. Many freshmen who seek interpretation have underlying counseling needs, and the MBTI is an "excuse" for them to make an appointment. In this way, the MBTI is a good counseling outreach and point of contact, however brief. Some students will have one session about their results and return months later to work on personal problems. Trust and mutual respect had been established in that first visit for MBTI results. Following the memo, when requests for appointments are high, I may group up to five students together for interpretation. Students do not seem to mind the small group and are invited to come back for further individual consultation if they so desire. I prefer individual interpretive appointments, when time allows, because of the better opportunity for exploration.

If students delay in obtaining their results for a year or two, caution should be used in interpretation because of the time laspe. There may be some change over time in the way students (or any individuals) report their Type. Although individuals' natural and innate Types haven't changed, such factors as increased self-awareness, transition stresses, and the break from parents can influence the way individuals **report** their preferences. Therefore, descriptions of the preference scales are checked out carefully against clients' self-perceptions and counselor observations. Students are offered the opportunity to retake the MBTI, especially if there is any doubt, or if preferences were mild or unclear. There has been some research on stability of preferences reported over time; several references are listed at the back of the book. There is some indication that one or more scales **may** be reported differently over the four year college cycle. Again, caution is necessary in utilizing old MBTI scores.

In the private practice of psychotherapy, I evaluate the appropriateness of MBTI administration on a case by case basis. I do not automatically administer the Indicator on first visit. I first make an initial assessment of the client's needs. The next section elaborates on criteria for using the MBTI. I follow the same approach when doing consultation, first making an assessment through interview and observation. Some practitioners use the MBTI for initial intake and information gathering, but my bias with all kinds of testing is to begin with face-to-face observation and interview.

Appropriate MBTI Use

Once I have made an initial assessment of the clients' needs and together we have formulated counseling goals, I will suggest use of the MBTI for the following kinds of issues and concerns:

— desire to explore career options and do life planning
— difficulty with a life/developmental passage or transition
— difficulty with interpersonal relationships and communications
— desire for self-exploration
— academic functioning and adjustment
— work functioning and performance
— leadership and organizational problems

The 18 cases in the next chapter will illustrate most of these applications.

The MBTI has value beyond the specific kinds of issues and concerns just listed. Its use can enhance the counseling process by:

— developing a common vocabulary and concepts for working with clients and their concerns;
— validating clients' perception of self;
— supporting clients' tentative life decisions;
— strengthening self-esteem and setting the direction for further self-development;
— providing an objective and concrete way to describe an emotionally loaded situation, such as a relationship conflict or work problem;
— offering a conceptual framework which aids clients to get a more objective view of themselves and their life situations, to view themselves from a fresh angle.

There are occasions when I don't believe the MBTI is appropriate. When the client is distrustful of therapists in general, of the counseling process, and of "tests", use should be deferred. There should be some rapport and client trust before the MBTI is introduced. Some clients are not good candidates for use because they are too hyperactive to take the Indicator, are too disturbed, or too paranoid. Just as with other kinds of tests and inventories, the practitioner must used good judgment. If counselors sense any client reluctance to participate in testing, this reluctance should be thoroughly, yet gently, explored before proceeding with test administration or interpretation. Inappropriate use, other than related to the nature of the client, will be discussed further under "Ethics of Use".

Introducing the MBTI to Clients

Given the above appropriate conditions for using the MBTI, clients should be introduced to the use of the MBTI in a way that makes sense to them in terms of mutually formulated counseling goals and their expressed needs. I suggest the MBTI and explain how it could be helpful to the counseling process at that point. I state what the MBTI can and cannot do. The MBTI is a tool for exploring personal strengths and preference. It will **not** point to a specific choice or direction. The results are not so definitive or specific that any counseling issues will be "solved" per se by knowing one's Type. A simple explanation can be given about how the results will relate to counseling goals. Examples are:

— in relationship counseling: "Knowing your preferences will help you to understand your style of communicating and how you may differ from your partner."
— in career counseling: "Understanding your preferences will help you to identify your strengths, how you might like to work, and what work settings might be satisfying to you."
— in academic counseling: "Your preferences will aid in identifying the ways you learn best as well as suggesting some learning skills you may wish to develop. We can use this information to formulate study approaches and choose appropriate academic courses."
— in counseling for mid-life transition: "Perhaps knowing your preferences will help us understand why you feel stuck at this point in your life and what you may need to feel satisfied."

Other points I usually cover are:

— the MBTI is not designed to be "tricky" or have trick questions.
— the MBTI is not a complex test designed to measure psychopathology, such as the MMPI.
— clients cannot "pass" or "fail".
— the instrument has been in use for a long time, with good information on reliability and validity (may have to explain these terms or use other language).
— I mention my experience using the MBTI in general terms.

Finally, I check for client questions about the MBTI and the willingness to participate.

Since the Indicator and *Manual* are both explicit about administration procedures, it is unnecessary to duplicate that information here. Most individual clients are given the question book and answer sheet to complete on their own at home. They are cautioned not to seek others' assistance in answering but to answer on their own in a non-distracting environment. The ideal, of course, is to have a quiet testing space at the counseling office. On occassion, I will require the client to complete the questions in my office or adjacent office, usually because of a poor home environment for test-taking. I tell clients who are tested individually that I will hand-score their answer sheets upon next visit (unless, of course, they drop the sheets off prior to the next appointment). Hand-scoring takes about five minutes.

A Model for Interpretation

At the time of interpretation, I begin with a restatement of what the MBTI results can and cannot do or reveal. I ask their reactions to answering the questions and give them opportunity to express frustration at the forced-choice items. This is also an opportunity to check on whether there were any unusual test-taking conditions or attitudes. Clients are reminded of the limitations of all self-reported inventories. I usually add that despite the self-reporting feature and possible "mood" at the time of answering the items, clients usually report surprise and agreement that Type descriptions "fit" them. Often clients report a sense of contradicting themselves in answering the questions. This can be explained by stating that because the instrument is measuring degree of preference on the various scales, there are several variations of the same question to discriminate how strongly the client feels about a certain response.

Often clients also express some confusion in answering the questions in one context such as work setting versus another context such as social/personal life. I explore this expressed discrepancy to clarify the client's meaning and then watch for specific discrepancies as we proceed to discuss the four preference scales. When clients claim a marked difference in the way they would answer in one context versus another, it may be helpful for the client to take the Indicator twice, each time with a particular setting in mind. This confusion seems to be more prevalent where scores are close to the middle on the scales. Generally I believe that people are consistent from one setting to another in expression of Type, but the possibility of this discrepancy should certainly be explored with clients and can be good material for counseling.

Discrepancy may also be signaled by differences in the scores on the word-pair section and on the phrases section of the Indicator. The scores from these two sections are recorded on the administrative side of the computer-scored printout. If a client with a slight preference for T scores as an F on the word-pairs and as a T on the phrases, there may be internal tension in regard to this judgment function. The counselor can explore this possibility.

The counseling goal is to increase clients' understanding of self, not to "fit" the client to a particular Type. Thus, when clients become frustrated with indefinite results, the counselor should stress the use of the results as more of a tool for exploration than an outcome in itself. Counselors should never force an outcome of a specific Type on clients, or create an expectation of clients needing clearly defined preferences. In the latter condition, clients may feel guilty or "wishy-washy", as several clients have termed themselves, for not having clear preferences. Clients who need closure and definitive answers (especially SJ's) can be encouraged to observe themselves, their behaviors and reactions, in a variety of situations in relation to the preference scales. This activity may bring about some clarification of Type. When clients are ready, they can retake the MBTI. Clients with indefinite results can be positively supported for being in an exploratory or transition phase involving growth and change, and encouraged to utilize counseling as an aid in this exploration.

The materials I use in interpretation vary but generally include:

— either the computer-scored printout or the hand-scored answer sheet
— "Understanding the Type Table" and/or *Introduction to Type*
— depending on the depth of interpretation, the books *Gifts Differing* and/or *Please Understand Me.*

The four preference scales will not be described here, since this is done thoroughly in sources mentioned previously. I would like to underscore the point, however, that clients should not view preference scores as skills, per se. Rather preferences can better be understood as broad strengths and tendencies to operate in certain ways that may lead to development of certain skills. For instance, a T preference does not signify a brilliantly analytical mind, although T does signify a desire to make judgments in a logical, analytical way. This desire could be developed into specific skills and abilities. It is important for clients to realize that their preferences do not exclude use of the opposite functions. Thus, having an F preference does not necessarily means that the client cannot periodically choose to function through logical analysis (T). The goal of developing all the functions over time needs to be reiterated

13

at a level appropriate to client comprehension. Interpretation is worded in dynamic, not static, terms with continuing reminders that there is individual variation within each Type.

There is some disagreement among practitioners and in the literature about how to interpret the strength of scores. Since the scales are basically dichotomous, as demonstrated by Myers in the *MBTI Manual*, the actual numerical score should not be very important. Therefore, an Extravert is an Extravert no matter what the numerical value. There are others who believe there is some significance to scores themselves, especially those that are very high or very low. When clients ask about the meaning of scores, some of the above information can be given, as appropriate. From years of clinical observation, I do believe that **ranges** of scores are usually significant. Many clinicians, including myself, view scores 9 and lower as tentative or slight preferences. Mild preferences are considered to be scores approximately in the 11-19 range, and strong preferences in the above 19 (to 59) range.

The counselor should be especially thorough in describing the characteristics of any scale with a slight preference. Using clear examples for each preference, counselors should explore where clients see themselves on that scale. Sometimes preferences may be stronger than reported scores reflect; this can be discovered through counseling exploration. Slight preferences may mean:

— a period of transition and experimentation with both functions;
— a lack of development of that function, perhaps for environmental reasons;
— an area of conflict, tension, or ambiguity;
— a reflection of attitude and mood the day of administration.

Slight preferences may reflect different dynamics in middle- or older-aged adults compared to adolescents and young adults. The latter are likely to be crystallizing preferences, perhaps shedding parental influences for emerging, yet still tentative, preferences of their own. Older adults with slight preferences may be working under conditions which force them to operate against their Types or may be undergoing major life style change, such as divorce. Again, the scale with the slight preference may reflect a tension within the client and in the client's life situation. The dynamic quality of the MBTI is apparent here, as well as the need to interpret results in the context of the client's life situation and age.

Beyond these general observations about the ranges of scores, actual numerical values, per se, do not seem that important in clinical use. The significance of scores in relation to level of client function has not been established in the research. However, my past observations of clients have led to "hunches" about the **possible** meaning of scores. The stronger the preference on a particular scale, the more likely those characteristics will influence coping and lifestyle in obvious ways. The stronger the preferences, the less likely Type seems to change on retest, although actual scores may vary somewhat. I do not assume, but rather explore the strong possibility that the strongly reported preferences are better developed functions than slight preferences. Sometimes a very strong preference may indicate a total, or almost total, avoidance of the opposite function. For example, an individual with a raw score of "0" for S and "23" for N had never balanced a checkbook and feared handling practical matters. In cases where the auxiliary function is a much stronger preference than the dominant, the counselor may wish to explore the meaning of this. This condition is more likely to occur with Introverts, because they use their auxiliary to deal with the outside world. This condition could also be a cautionary signal that a slight preference for E-I or J-P scales may not represent true preference and may account for the wrong functions being designated as dominant and auxiliary. Again, these are areas to explore with clients without putting them under pressure to BE any particular Type. Discussion of MBTI results should be process oriented, not outcome oriented.

Some clients may ask, "Isn't it better to be in the middle, so I can use both functions, 50-50?" My usual response is: Type theory indicates that individuals usually develop strong preferences over time, and having a strong preference does **not** mean one cannot utilize the opposite function or attitude. In fact, a goal of personal growth is eventually to be able to use all the functions as needed in particular situations. Generally, it appears to be easier for people to function when they are clear about their preferences. There is generally less tension, even when called upon to use the less-preferred function or attitude in a specific situation.

The language used in interpretation should be appropriate to the educational level **and** the Type of the client. If a client prefers Sensing, for example, vocabulary of a concrete, less abstract nature might be more conducive to comprehension. Non-biased descriptions and careful avoidance of value-laden words are crucial. Counselor tone needs to be respectful and objective. Counselors will have to monitor their explanations and listen for biases or "favorites" implied in their interpretations. Sometimes clients get the impression that one preference is more desirable than another. This impression should be corrected by asking the client for reaction or feedback after explanation of a scale and results. If clients seem disappointed with the interpretation, counselors may have presented the preferences in a biased fashion, or clients may have misunderstood explanations. (Their disappointment could also signal their inaccurate reporting of preferences on the Indicator.)

15

After explanation of the four scales, I demonstrate how the four preferences combine to form one of 16 possible Types, illustrating the dynamic aspects of Type. Clients are asked their reactions to this information. Results are then related to the ongoing counseling process and goals. I might ask the client, "Does this have meaning for you in relation to...?" Finally, I may share my Type with the client to promote an atmosphere of equal-to-equal collaboration and to illustrate any differences. Mutual self-disclosure is usually helpful, but there may be clients and situations where that disclosure might confuse or intimidate the client. The same guidelines of self-disclosure for general counseling apply here.

Type Considerations in Interpretation

My clinical experiences with the MBTI suggest varying the interpretation process somewhat to meet the needs of different Types. Some of the more prominent differences are worth mentioning here. When working with clients with a strong preference for Introversion, the interpretation process flows very differently than with Extraverts. Introverts will take in all the information about their Type and perhaps ask a few clarifying questions. They will not, however, frequently interrupt with questions and comments, as most Extraverts are prone to do. Also, the Introverts need some time "to digest" the results before responding to them. Usually Introverts appreciate some time to consider before asking questions or discussing personal relevance; therefore, a follow-up appointment for this purpose is recommended. The Extraverts, however, may move quickly into discussion of MBTI relevance to their lives, sometimes not allowing enough time to really consider the implications of the various scales. It seems easier to overload an Introvert with too much information than an Extravert. Also the E's may prefer a faster paced discussion. The counselor may need to pause more often and wait for the introverted clients to formulate comments or questions in the silence. The counselor must take care to solicit feedback from highly introverted clients to make sure there is understanding. The E's will show signs of understanding or confusion more readily by their frequent comments. Of course, the counselor's Type is also a factor here. As an Extravert, I need to be careful to slow myself down with introverted clients and allow enough pauses.

Another interpretation difference involves Sensing and Intuition. S Types seem to prefer descriptive phrases and comments written out on their answer sheet or on other MBTI materials used. Examples from daily life are especially welcomed by the S's, I usually write out some sequential steps that follow from the MBTI results. These steps might look like: (a) summary of strengths, (b) potential career areas to explore, (c) first step to exploration (e.g. interview a person in the profession), (d) second step to exploration, and so forth. While many Intuitives will ask about patterns, possibilities, and theory involved in the MBTI, S's are generally more interested in the immediate applications. Many NP's like to apply the MBTI to career planning through brainstorming and divergent thinking, but the SJ's become frustrated by divergent thinking. Usually they do not want career options expanded but rather desire convergence to fewer options. Good career counseling includes both divergent and convergent aspects, but the counselor will need to be sensitive to the tolerance levels for divergent and convergent thinking of the different Types.

Another interesting difference is between Thinking and Feeling preferences. Often T's will want data to substantiate implications of the Indicator. They may even ask about reliability and validity. T's tend to be more skeptical about the instrument. If the counselor is an MBTI enthusiast, it is important not to brush off the T's skepticism, but rather to work with it by sharing information/data in the *Manual* and other MBTI materials as appropriate. Feeling Types tend to become impatient with much data and are more likely to personalize results. An important distinction should be made in interpreting the meaning of the T-F scale. The counselor should be clear with the client that Thinking preference does not mean clients don't have feelings, or vice versa, that F's can't think logically or think at all. Rather, the counselor should stress that this scale is a reflection of two different rational processes, which use different criteria for making decisions/judgments. T's place a higher priority on objective facts; F's on interpersonal issues or subjective factors. These distinctions, with an emphasis on the client's priority of criteria for evaluation, are important ones.

Ethics of Use

All counselors and therapists have a code of ethics developed by their professions which include guidelines for ethical use of test materials. These general ethics apply, of course, to using the MBTI.

The most important and obvious of these are standardized administration and confidentiality. The MBTI should be used according to instructions on the booklet and in the *Manual*. This means, for instance, that specific questions should not be lifted from the Indicator to get a "quick reading" on a particular preference scale. It also means the instrument should be used on appropriate populations and results utilized as suggested in the *Manual*. Confidentiality seems to have become more of an issue with the recent increased use of the MBTI. Results should be available only to clients unless they give permission for that informtion to be released to a third party. Often in the college setting, faculty, advisors, or others concerned about a student's welfare will ask about MBTI results. The confidential nature of results can be explained tactfully and the staff encouraged to discuss with the individual student their interest in learning MBTI results. Students may want to share their results with their advisors or others. In some cases, coaches and teachers have requested that their teams and classes sign a list to release their MBTI results. Since there may be a very subtle form of coercion here, I discourage this approach. For example, it would be hard for a young student to refuse her coach's request to sign a release after the coach said the the information would improve teamwork. My alternative to these requests is that coaches/teachers supply me with the names of those in the group interested in their results; then I will do a group interpretation and deliver results directly to each student. Activities can be structured in the group for sharing information related to teamwork, learning styles, or other issues. Students are in control of their results and the amount of information they choose to disclose. Coaches, teachers, or other staff involved with these groups are encouraged to share their MBTI Types in these group activities, so a collaborative atmosphere is developed.

The confidentiality issue is a powerful one in private consulting as well. Employers have approached me about using the MBTI as a screening instrument for hiring and promotion. I have always declined and have tried to educate employers about a more constructive use of Type information. The ethical and more effective use of the instrument occurs after the employee is functioning in an organization. Then Type can be related to strengths, functions, team building, and professional development. When consulting with business groups, the same approach can be used as with student groups: a group explanation of MBTI and results given directly to the individuals, not to administrators or supervisors.

In addition to a general code of ethics for test use, a few other issues bear mentioning here. One is interpretive bias. Some users not thoroughly familiar with the MBTI or unaware of their own Type biases may slant interpretation or send messages that a particular preference is "good" or "not desirable". There is also the danger in over-generalizing results and implying that all people of a certain Type behave the same way. A second issue is assuring that accurate and sufficient information about results has been provided and that clients have had opportunity to ask questions and clear up confusions. Short-hand labels and over-simplification to save time are misuses of the MBTI.

A third ethical concern is the client's reaction to test results. If the client disagrees with results and doesn't believe they are accurate, the counselor should not impose the results on the client or become defensive, but rather should explore the perceived differences and help clients to be comfortable with themselves.

Finally, there are those awkward situations when a new MBTI enthusiast asks to take the MBTI question book home to administer to spouse, friend, roommate, etc. These enthusiasts are anxious to learn the Type of their significant other and think they know enough to explain results. A few times in the past I have conceded to this, but I am becoming more and more convinced that there are too many risks with this. The enthusiast does not have the skill to be objective and thorough in translating results. Also, this may become a power issue in a relationship. Some underlying coercion or some hidden agenda might be present. My response is to state my belief in giving results directly to the individual tested; we arrange some way to do this.

Although there probably are other ethical concerns, these points were chosen to cover the basic ethics as well as the issues I have had to grapple with in my practice. This chapter has laid a foundation for the cases that follow by discussing appropriate settings and client populations for using the MBTI, as well as interpretation issues. Furthermore, attention to the ethics of use is crucial to safeguarding client rights and professionalism within counseling, therapy, and consultation.

Chapter IV
EIGHTEEN CASES

The core of this casebook, of course, is the clinical vignettes in this chapter. Eighteen cases have been chosen from my college and private counseling practices. Although client ages range from 18-45, a majority of the cases are young adults. Selection was made on the following basis:

— to represent all 16 Types and two other Type conditions;
— to present a frequently occurring personal problem of each Type;
— to include approximately equal numbers of men and women.

The cases describe the client's presenting problem and demonstrate how the MBTI was used in identifying client's developmental needs, strengths and weaknesses. The cases also illustrate how the MBTI can help in formulating counseling goals and interventions. Although the cases chosen demonstrate the kinds of problems frequently seen in counseling for each Type, one should not generalize that certain problems are inherent to certain Types.

Some cases represent brief therapy, one or two sessions in duration, and other cases reflect counseling contact over longer periods, up to several years. To keep cases brief and focused on MBTI applications in counseling, other counseling particulars unrelated to this casebook goal have been excluded. Counselors will know from their own practices that case descriptions do not capture all that transpires in their interactions with clients. Also, as reflected in actual practice, some of the clients described here were unwilling to commit to ongoing counseling and only wanted the "bandaid approach".

As each case is presented, that Type will be shown in the upper corner with dominant and auxiliary functions, as well as third and fourth, indicated. Also an "I" will indicate that the function is introverted; an "E" will signal that the function is extraverted.

Dan - INFJ
Two "Personalities", One Career Decision

Dan was a sophomore referred by his academic advisor, who had sensed some emotional issues behind Dan's expressed interest in transferring to another college. Dan was uncomfortable mentioning the transfer, because this would be his third college within a two year period. He described his situation as a general "lack of motivation" to do his academic work. His analysis was that this particular college environment wasn't the "right one" for him and that when he found the right environment, he would "get motivated". In other words, Dan was looking for motivation from some external source. Dan had not chosen an academic major yet and had no career direction. He did feel strongly that he wanted to be in college at this time. He was bewildered about his lack of motivation and his paralysis in trying to make decisions about his future.

Dan felt much pressure from family members to major in something that would be "useful" and to make a career choice that would have high financial gain and status. He was the youngest of three brothers and felt a need to match their achievements. His father was a top executive with a prestigious corporation; his mother was a homemaker.

Dan's interests were vague. He thought he might like the social sciences but wasn't sure whether this was due to an older brother's influence. He also liked a political science course he had taken and he liked to write.

After obtaining background information from Dan, we discussed the issues of motivation and decision making. He was able to articulate his need to establish a meaningful goal in his life. He chose to take two inventories to help with identifying a goal—the MBTI and the Strong-Campbell Interest Inventory (SCII).

During the next session we reviewed his MBTI results. Dan had well-defined preferences for INFJ. As we explored the meaning of these scales, he became much more animated and hopeful than previously. We spoke in general terms about career clusters that utilized the strengths of the INFJ (communications, counseling,

21

teaching, writing, etc.) but planned to postpone focusing more specifically until after SCII results were also reviewed.

Surprisingly, the SCII results, reviewed in the third session, were quite different from what one would expect from an INFJ and from statements Dan had made in the initial interview. Dan scored high on Conventional and Enterprising. The Conventional theme reflects desire for tradition and structure and liking for office practice, defined tasks, and work in large, structured organizations. The Enterprising theme includes interests in leading, selling, persuading, public speaking, usually in business, public, or organizational settings.

I have found that INFJ's and NF's in general usually score higher on the themes of Artistic and Social of the SCII. An INFJ may occasionally score high on the Investigative theme as well. These differences between the MBTI and SCII, plus differences from interview information, indicated to me some discrepancies in Dan's perceptions and the possibility of some strong internal conflicts. I have formed the opinion through years of utilizing these inventories, that the MBTI will reflect the "truer" self, and the SCII will reflect a more superficial view of self and pershaps the identification phenomenon. By "identification" I mean the mechanism of taking for one's own, various interests and characteristics seen in those one admires and respects. Therefore, counseling intervention focused on exploring these discrepancies between self-reported conventional, structured interests and a creative, expressive individualistic self.

When gently questioned about these apparent discrepancies, Dan animatedly identified these two "sides" of himself as "three-piece suit" and "true self". Three-piece suit represented his father's lifestyle—financial and psychological security, respectability, adulthood, etc. This was the only view of adulthood he had had growing up. In his upper middle class, suburban childhood every adult male on his block wore a three-piece suit, carried a briefcase, and worked as an executive in a large organization. He described his true self as not liking structure, creative, emotional, unexpressed, and "in hiding" from people, because people like his father wouldn't understand this self. Using a Gestalt Therapy approach, Dan was encouraged to create a dialogue between his two "sides". Hearing this dialogue he was able to clarify thoughts and feelings associated with these two sides of polarities. He could then see how he had become "stuck" about school and careers. His true self was afraid to grow up if adulthood meant "three-piece suit"; thus he moved from school to school and was not goal oriented. Dan was metaphorically "dragging his feet" to slow down the process of movement toward adulthood. Yet, he was unable to let go of the three-piece suit because of the security and

22

familiarity of that model. Also as a strong Feeling Type, he feared family disapproval, especially from his father, if he did not pursue the three-piece suit direction. It was very important to "belong" in his family and to please his parents.

Thus, Dan was torn by the internal pull of these polarities. Through several sessions utilizing Gestalt Therapy, he was able to integrate aspects of both poles and realize that he needed and could use aspects of both. Based on his expressed interests, test results, and discussion, several career areas emerged which Dan decided to explore: sports psychology/coaching and political science directed toward public administration. Sports psychology could utilize his NF strengths: empathy, desire to motivate people, tendency to see possibilities and to innovate. This career field would also provide structure with some security and status. Public administration might utilize his potential as a leader/manager. INFJ's tend to be sympathetic, conscientious, and organized. Although our work together did not establish a final direction, it did free Dan up to begin moving forward. Energy that had been tied up in this internal struggle was now available for school and decision making. He became motivated. The MBTI was valuable in this case for quickly identifying unexpressed aspects of self and providing an objective structure and vocabulary for discussing this self. Reliance solely on an interest inventory for career and life planning would have given a false picture in which the true conflict would not have emerged. Dan did transfer to a larger university which had academic programs related to his interests in sports psychology and public administration. He planned to continue career and personal counseling there.

INTROVERTED FEELING
with Intuition
INFP
F
N
S
T

George - INFP
Unemployed Minister

George sought career counseling after being unemployed for a length of time. At mid-life he found himself discouraged and full of self-doubts. He wanted to "find a new direction" for his life. A personal history revealed the following:

— A multi-disciplinary undergraduate degree in political science, history, and social science;
— A master's degree from a divinity school;
— Some years in the militray service during which he reported the most interesting work had been night time reconnaissance missions in Vietnam (because of the challenge, "need to be alert", surprise elements, and lack of structure);
— Original plan to pursue a career in missionary work thwarted because of health problems of a family member;
— Desire to have his own church but unsuccessful in obtaining a church appointment during the four years since graduate school;
— Since graduate school, odd jobs such as building maintenance.

From George's history it became apparent that George had a serious conflict between his longing for a career in the church and his need to find a secure job. He wondered if he should retrain in some other career area, such as computers, because of his failure to find a job in the ministry. Through the counseling process, then, the pivotal question emerged: should he rigorously pursue career possibilities related to the church, or should he explore other career options? George decided upon reflection that he wasn't ready to give up his aspirations for work in the church, since he had felt "called by God", and this goal remained an important one for him.

I suggested he take the MBTI so that we would have a clearer idea of what his strengths were. I told him that research had been done with the MBTI and clergy. His results might suggest certain job functions and settings. MBTI results might also give us ideas on how to structure his job search. The MBTI is often a "check and blance" to information and perceptions derived from personal interviews. Where discrepancies emerge between results and reported interests, strengths, etc., further exploration of these areas should be done. Where there is substantial agreement between results and the interview, the client feels validated. George agreed to take the MBTI and return for a second, interpretive session.

George's preferences, INFP, were all well-defined. The preference scales were explained to him in detail using examples drawn from interview information of the previous session and showing career applications for each scale. Some behavioral examples of his INFP preferences were:

— His diverse interest in academic subjects as an undergraduate and his difficulty in focusing on any one academic major (INP);
— His penchant for digressing during the sessions into discussions of patterns and trends in religious thinking; he loved theory and new ideas (N). I pointed out to him that he had preferences similiar to those of college professors and others working in an academic environment;
— His unwillingness to compromise his strong religious and personal beliefs in terms of the type of church he was willing to serve. These beliefs were adhered to even in the face of "hard, cold economic facts" and practicalities (F; I frequently find this uncompromising quality among INFP's);
— His lack of persistence in the job search, lack of enterprising behavior necessary to find a job, and his turning inward with discouragement. He was stuck or paralyzed at this point in his life. Often INFP's and INTP's become easily thwarted, do not persist when obstacles block their paths, and prefer to change their original goals rather than to struggle with obstacles.

This latter characteristic was discussed in great depth with George so that he could understand and express feelings related to his current situation. Ways of confronting obstacles and persisting, instead of withdrawing, were discussed. One suggestion was to act "out-of-character" by designing a weekly plan of job search activities with specific tasks for each day. He must complete these activities in a "professional" manner. As an INFP, he was likely to put off job search efforts and wait for something to "fall into his lap". Also, negative responses from prospective employers could send George back into discouraged withdrawal unless he had promised himself to follow his "professional" plan day by day. He was encouraged to hold before him the image of the goal he was seeking in the church, and when he became discouraged, to view this goal (taking advantage of his NF ability for visual imagery). I have found INFP's can persist when the goal is personally meaningful and well-defined.

After discussing these internal dynamics, we again looked at his career strengths in terms of the MBTI. Some of these were:

— ability to listen and consider thoroughly and empathically (INF);
— patience with theory and love of complexity (IN);
— imagination and creativity (N);
— ability to see patterns and possibilities in people situations (NF);
— quiet warmth and caring (IF);
— strong faith and belief in values (NF);
— flexibility (P).

These strengths were then applied to the job search.

The last phase of our session focused on work settings, job functions, résumés, and how to talk about his strengths in interviews using the MBTI formulations. Pastoral counseling emerged as a strong interest; a large percentage of INFP's are attracted to this occupation. Other interests were campus ministry, editing religious publications, work in religious publishing houses, and Christian education. George also planned to pursue more systematically the possibility of his own church. We discussed his possible avoidance of fundraising and "nitty-gritty" budget management aspects of having his own church. He might want to examine a prospective church to see if others on the church staff would work in those capacities. George could also emphasize to church interviews that his strengths were in preaching, teaching, and counseling (as opposed to fundraising and organization). We brainstormed a list of contacts and potential employers. At the end of the session George said he planned to throw himself into these job search efforts and would get back with me if he found himself discouraged or stuck. He realized there was much for him to do and was challenged by this.

The MBTI was especially helpful in validating George's strengths at a time in mid-life when he experienced great self-doubt and discouragement. He was helped to understand the intrapersonal dynamics which prevented him from meeting his goals and learned some ways of overcoming or changing his way of coping. He left these two sessions with a more positive outlook and improved self-esteem. This was a case of brief therapy with no further contact, although George was encouraged to continue counseling if he met with any difficulties.

Carol - INxP
The Inability to Evaluate

Carol was a 40 year old divorced woman who sought counseling for her depression and confusion. She described her depression as an overwhelming sense of discouragement and helplessness about facing decisions and dealing with life. Carol felt paralyzed, in "a fog", unable to discern the "real" from her "inner conceptualizations". Carol added that she wasn't in touch with her "true self". She stated that different people saw different images of her, leading her to wonder if there was one true image/self.

The MBTI was suggested as one of the many counseling tools to aid her in getting in touch with her true self and secondarily to aid her in making impending lifestyle choices (career change, relocations, etc.). Her results, INxP, were strong preferences on all scales except the Thinking-Feeling scale, where she was in the middle.

Her auxiliary function, Intuition, was well-developed. As an Introvert, she used her auxiliary function to interact with the outside world. In fact, she had developed Intuition to such an extent that she was regarded as an extremely gifted student and creative writer. Many viewed her as abstract, intellectual, and imaginative. This strong Intuition, however, led her to perceive every issue as complex and multi-faceted. No decision or event could be interpreted simply; Carol often tied herself up in mental knots. There was no balance of Intuition with Thinking or Feeling.

Thinking or Feeling should have been her dominant function based on the INxP combination. Yet her score on this scale was in the middle. Introverts use their dominant function within themselves, as opposed to with the external world. Consequently, Introverts may develop their auxiliaries before their dominant functions, since they need a tool for interacting with the environment. Assuming the scores were an accurate description of her stage of Type development, one could specualte on additional reasons why Carol had not developed her dominant function (T or F). She had a miserable and bizarre childhood, impacted by an alcoholic parent. At a very early age, she had resorted to daydreaming, fantasizing, and looking at bitter realities from novel or humorous angles. She had worked hard to avoid evaluating or having contact with feelings or personal responses to her environment. Finally, she had been so good at using Intuition as a child in school, that she had received external rewards and recognition which reinforced this preference.

One of the goals of therapy, in terms of an MBTI framework, was to help her learn to access her evaluative or judging function and develop either Thinking or Feeling. In developing this function, she could get a better sense of self by having a way to evaluate outside stimuli, possibilities, events in relation to her "self" criteria.

Much of the above formulation was shared with the client over several sessions. One of the therapeutic goals we agreed upon was to learn to access one of the evaluative functions and experiment with this. Interventions were chosen to facilitate her going inside and inventorying Thinking or Feeling criteria. My approach drew primarily from Gestalt Therapy and values clarification techniques. Other helpful modalities were a system Gendlin (1981) developed called "focusing", meditation, and guided imagery.

For example, Carol would be asked to suspend talking and cognitive inner "chatter" and search deep inside herself for some place of awareness or "knowing". She was encouraged to use simple descriptive words to observe sensory impressions and body awareness. She was discouraged and interrupted from shifting to intuitive speculation and theorizing. Carol had to exert much effort to be aware of herself in an immediate, sensory way. Her process was that as she got close to an emotion, she immediately skirted it, rushing back to a cognitive state. Coping with Intuition was so well established that she continuously attempted to shift back to that mode. Therapy required gentle but firm persistence and redirection to utilize her other functions.

Values clarification techniques were utilized to help her explore the whole process of identifying an important criterion/value, examining its origins and implications for behavior, etc. Again, Carol often attempted to rely on Intuition and produced an extremely complicated, confusing theorization. She needed to be redirected to stay on track.

Meditation approaches were particularly helpful, because these assisted her to go inside and get in touch with her physical and spiritual selves. She was instructed in deep breathing and relaxation exercises. Guided imagery was occasionally added, such as imagining climbing a mountain and meeting a wise being who spoke to her. The guided imagery harnessed her Intuition in the service of accessing Thinking or Feeling.

Through several months of weekly sessions, she explored her inner self and her evaluative process. She began to identify with the Feeling function and to learn how to access that function. She realized how she often "protected" herself from experiencing pain or discomfort by playing on Intuition. She felt a "split" in the past between her "head" and her "body" but now began to experience herself as a "whole solid self".

This new awareness of her own process was then applied to impending life decisions. Although she still was somewhat uncomfortable making decisions, she felt more confident in making them with her newly discovered evaluative function, Feeling. By using techniques and processes learned in these counseling sessions, she now knew how to get in touch with her inner nature/needs/values to sort out choices that were appropriate for her. She found herself with more energy and no longer depressed. Long after our counseling relationship was terminated, she wrote to say she had made several important life decisions—marriage, career, and relocation. Her letter reflected her positive outlook.

Toni - ENFP
Playing Versus Achievement

The scoring printout from CAPT says in its final paragraph about the ENFP:

> If their judgment is undeveloped, they may commit themselves to ill-chosen projects, fail to finish anything, and squander their inspirations, abilities, and energy on irrelevant, half-done jobs. At their worst, they are unstable, undependable, fickle, and easily discouraged.

This cautionary statement applies to a number of the young adult ENFP's with whom I've worked. When their auxiliary, F, s undeveloped, these individuals may appear as "busy bees" or "social butterflies", extending themselves way beyond their physical limits and often developing stress-related illnesses or exhaustion. Sometimes they exhibit hysterical behavior—physical agitation, emotionalism, rapid speech, chaotic gestures. Mood swings may be extreme: periods of overextension/activity followed by exhaustion, discouragement, and sometimes depression. In contrast, ENFP's with a developed balancing function, F, are also highly energetic, active with people and activities, and expressive, but usually are able to take on appropriate work loads and keep activity at a manageable level. They are more likely to withdraw periodically to "refuel" and evaluate.

Toni is an example of an ENFP with undeveloped Judgment. Toni sought counseling near the end of her freshman year in college. She was doing poorly in her pre-med classes, feeling unmotivated to study, guilty, and experiencing much conflict with her family. At the same time, she admitted to an extremely active social life involving drinking, smoking pot, and late partying on school nights. She was a whirlwind of social activity.

Initial counseling goals were to help her to clarify her present situation, to express related feelings, and to learn to manage her time and achieve a better balance between academics and social life. The MBTI was introduced as a way to look at her learning style and preferences that might illuminate the way she was coping with college life. Her MBTI results were available from freshman class testing; we reviewed these results during the second session. Scales were described thoroughly with their implications for learning, studying approaches, academic strengths, and potential weaker areas. She had strong preferences for ENP, and mild preference for F.

Toni lacked awareness of her feelings and their influence on her behavior. A Gestalt approach was employed to help her access these feelings. She was asked to imagine her mother present in the room and talk with her about the current conflict. As feelings emerged, Toni was assisted in identifying these and exploring them further. She needed some coaching to utilize and understand her Feeling function. Her auxiliary "F" was not yet well-developed and might be called primitive. She had never taken the time to suspend external activity to introvert and listen to her inner function.

Through this imagined dialogue with her mother, Toni also became aware that she had a strong conflict or tension between two poles which she identified as "the achiever" and "the player". On the other hand, she was stimulated and excited about the sciences and learning in general. On the other hand, she rebelled against structure, organization, the "have-to's" of homework; she desired a playful, free-spirited existence. This latter attitude is often seen in EP Types. My role was to help her understand these two sides of herself and how this tension between the two impacted her daily life. In Gestalt theory the individual works towards integration of elements of both poles, since both poles represent vital elements of the self. She was encouraged to use her Feeling function to evaluate what was really important to her. In addition to Gestalt approaches, such as dialogue between her playful and achieving selves, she was encouraged to find daily quiet time "to go inside" and to keep a stream-of-consciousness journal. Journal writing may not always come naturally to high Extraverts, but is a good way to slow them down to use introverted Feeling.

At this early point in our work together, she was not ready to take responsibility for her choices and behaviors. It was also apparent that she needed continuing counseling to assist in development of her auxiliary function. Over a period of months, she vacillated between wanting to change her lifestyle and resisting taking charge. She blamed circumstances, her friends, and family, and felt buffeted by fate and "controlled" by time. I challenged her to identify her own feelings and needs and evaluate behaviors on that basis; in other words, to take charge instead of just reacting. The P preference often involves this attitude of being at the mercy of fate.

Toni blamed friends because she couldn't say no to requests or invitations. Often Feeling Types have this difficulty because of the need for harmony and approval. We worked on assertiveness techniques for saying no and on her being able to use her auxiliary to answer the questions: "What is it I need at this moment? What is important to me?" Like most NF's, relationships were of prime importance to her. If her relationships weren't going well, school-work seemed inconsequential to her. She needed assertiveness and interpersonal skills to help her achieve balance in her life. When her relationships were more satisfying, she concentrated on her studies.

During the first few months I worked with Toni, her academic performance was up and down. She would express intentions of getting organized, work with a burst of energy, then avoid work, socialize and party to exhaustion. Toni, like many ENFP's, had initial bursts of enthusiasm and energy toward her courses and assignments but then did not follow through. We continued to work on issues of priorities taking responsibility for her behavior, and controlling her own life. She did not need techniques on **how** to organize herself and **how** to study; in the counseling sessions she could demonstrate awareness of these behavior. What defeated her periodically was her own inner conflict and the lack of committment to use these techniques. Thus, counseling interventions continued to be directed towards these internal conflicts and emotions.

These interventions gradually led to improved use of her Feeling function, better understanding of herself, and a more balanced life-style. Toni changed her major to English and felt more satisfied with herself and her school performance. She loved literature and writing and was better able to sustain academic interest than in the sciences. Understanding her preferences for ENFP suggested the above counseling approach and a plan for personal development. I lost contact with Toni following her successful completion of college.

Jesse - ISFJ
A Struggle for Independence

Jesse exemplifies many clients who are young, usually female, non-assertive, and struggling with dependency issues. Frequently these clients have a profile which is ISFJ. Many ISFJ clients seek prolonged counseling or therapy and expect the therapist to direct or even parent them. In comparing my private practice with that of several other psychotherapists, it seems that this profile may be more true for young adult clients but extends to many ISFJ's in mid-life as well. Therapists must be careful not to "feed" this dependency in long-term counseling relationships.

Jesse sought counseling early in her college career because she felt depressed. She was a "slow" learner by her own definition, and was working very hard "just to earn C's". She had difficulty grasping abstract concepts, an essential requirement of most of her college course work. She had not become involved with her peers. Jesse was the youngest of three, the "baby" of the family, and still dependent on other family members for decision making. She quickly became impatient with herself and with any sort of complexity (in academic or life situations). Jesse saw herself as "dumb". She took herself very seriously, with little sense of humor or ability to get outside herself and get another perspective.

Jesse expected me to give her specific direction or "how-to's" for coping with college. She became confused when I was non-directive and also when I shifted from her focus on concrete daily problems to exploration of the patterns of her coping. She could not relate to metaphors or imagery activities. Furthermore, Jesse had much difficulty generalizing a discreet piece of learning about herself in a given situation to other situations. As an ENFP, I had to work consciously to approach interventions in a more structured, concrete manner, so that I could "join" with her and not leave her confused.

Jesse had very strong preferences for ISFJ. These results were interpreted in such a way as to acknowledge her strengths and formulate some counseling goals for academic adjustment using MBTI concepts. Some of the strengths to be utilized in coping were: conscientiousness (ISJ), caring and personal warmth (IF), persistence and organization (J). A mutually agreed upon goal was to use not only the strengths of her preferences but also to develop her less-preferred functions. Counseling sessions were structured with these specific goals, mutually established:

— to develop other learning strategies to handle college courses;
— to work towards independence and making her own decisions;
— to learn assertive behavior;
— to become more playful and flexible.

The learning approach natural to those with ISFJ preferences was explained along with discussion of other learning approaches necessary to handle college work. As an ISFJ, she was deliberate, thorough, and therefore often slower than many other Types. ISFJ's are often slower readers, focusing on one word at a time. Reading skills development for them include teaching them to scan and group words to increase speed. Jesse also preferred learning in a hands-on (S), practical (S), personal (F), linear (S) and structured (J) way. Almost all of her professors were N, and most were NT (I had tested faculty during an MBTI workshop). The existing differences in teaching and learning styles were discussed. The N professors generally taught in a global, non-sequential way, without showing how theories and ideas were connected. An S prefers to learn by building to a theory with step-by-step information (linear). An N prefers to learn by seeing the theory or "big picture" first and then several examples to illustrate the theory (global). S's often become frustrated with global teachers who "jump" from concept to concept. N's often become bored with teachers who are deliberate and systematic in presenting detailed information. Thinking professors were generally more impersonal than Jesse liked and was used to in high school. Although she would continue to favor learning with Sensing and Feeling, she could develop the ability to utilize her Intuition for abstraction and her Thinking for anlaysis. Plans were made for her to attend the Learning Skills Center to improve reading speed, comprehension, and study skills. Jesse was encouraged to see herself as not less intelligent than others but rather in need of different ways to learn in college.

ISFJ's often have difficulty saying no to people's requests and are very concerned about harmony. Furthermore, they may have a tendency to internalize anger. These characteristics are strong factors in many of the depressed ISFJ clients I see, particularly female clients, who generally are more socialized to internalized anger. Jesse usually took the blame or responsibility for any interpersonal conflict and did not express angry or hurt feelings. Assertiveness training through individual and later group counseling developed her communication skills in these areas. These skills helped her to assert herself with family, and she began to make her own decisions. Change was slow in coming, since Jesse was apprehensive about change and not willing to take risks; she held on to the old and familiar.

In regard to change, if I pushed her too quickly or too hard to try a new behavior, she would resist and cling to the old way more determinedly. Many ISJ Types will respond this way to growth/ change oriented therapists. Our relationship was a series of gentle pushes, cautious tries, and sometimes retreats. Occasionally I would take the other tack and suggest, paradoxically, that she wasn't "ready" for a particular change and should be "more cautious", "go slower". Then Jesse's response was to move forward without resisting the suggestion.

Most difficult for her was accessing her playful, spontaneous "child" within. She was safer with careful, considered structure and serious endeavor. Yet she described her life as dull and devoid of fun. As she developed more trust in me and more faith in herself to try new behaviors, I was able to coax her into more playful behaviors. Exaggeration of a rigid behavior was one way she was able to laugh at herself. Another approach was to ask her to de- scribe a time in childhood when she was mischievious or had fun; the description was used to help her access playful feelings. Some- times we playfully brainstormed "out-of-character" things she could do. Then her homework was to try one of these things and note her reaction and reactions of others to her. Again, Jesse always needed some kind of structure for her growth and the counseling sessions.

In helping her develop her Intuition and see the broader patterns of her behaviors, I used very concrete metaphors at first, such as driving a car. Shifting gears was analagous to adapting, and the gears were MBTI functions. Over a period of several years, Jesse gained insight into herself and her coping patterns.

Sessions spanned several years but were not continuous. Rather, particular issues were worked on, followed by time away from counseling to practice new learnings. This periodic counseling prevented intense dependency on me. She became depressed much less often and less severely and recognized when she was being im- patient with herself. I also learned from Jesse to be more patient. Her way of growing and changing was very different from what I naturally preferred. Mutual respect and fascination with each other's processes were important elements in our counseling relationship.

There is a cheerful postscript. Jesse called me long after gradua- tion to share her enthusiasm about her elementary teaching job. She was living on her own and feeling quiet confident and competent. She described several teaching incidents where she had used her other functions to work creatively and flexibly with the children. And she said, "I'm starting back to graduate school part time!"

The Roommate Conflict - ISFJ vs ENFP

The resident aide in the dormitory had tried to resolve emerging conflicts between two freshman women. When the conflicts continued, she referred the students to me. They came in together and expressed an interest in resolving their differences and the tension. They said they basically liked and enjoyed each other and wanted to stay friends, but their differences in values and life styles were getting in the way. They wanted me to "arbitrate", to say who was "right" and who was "wrong".

The ISFJ (Mary) was the more upset. She complained that Lana (ENFP) was giving their room and consequently herself a bad reputation by bringing "lots of guys" to the room. Mary felt judged by others in the living unit for associating with someone labeled by some others as "loose". Although she wanted to do things with Lana, she was reluctant because of this issue. She called herself an "old-fashioned" person who believed in dating one person at a time and reserving sexual intimacy for marriage. Furthermore, she felt thrown off balance when Lana invited friends without telling her in advance. Mary had a strong belief that the room should be a place of refuge and security. She could not understand Lana's behavior.

Lana, on the other hand, expressed hurt feelings and frustration at not being accepted by Mary. She said she was willing to accept Mary as she was, but felt as if Mary was trying to "impose her moral values" and social style on Lana. Lana's attitude was, "Everyone should do their own thing".

After initial discussion of their perceptions of the problem, we began to examine differences using the MBTI, which all freshmen had taken during orientation. Each scale was explained, with specific references and examples related to their conflicts. The MBTI was presented as a tool to look at differences in preferences for dealing with the world, people, things around them and differences in values. Also conveyed were the following:

— All freshmen take the MBTI so that we can use the information to assist in academic and career planning, in improving reading and study skills, and generally in assisting students with self-exploration and understanding.

— I have used the MBTI in past years to assist roommates, close friends, couples, families, and people who work together to understand differences in style, so they can appreciate strengths and not view differences as conflict directed at them personally.

Some of the most relevant aspects of differences revealed by the MBTI scales and discussed with Mary and Lana were:

On the Introvert (I)—Extravert (E) Scale: Mary (I) needed quiet space and sanctuary and had a lower tolerance than Lana to traffic in the room. Lana preferred many social contacts and had a lower need for privacy than Mary.

On the Sensing (S)—Intuition (N) Scale: Mary (S) held strong traditonal views and was initially unable to see other possible value systems or to see the world through Lana's eyes. Lana, with her Intuition, challenged traditional views and looked for new possibilities in life-style and friendships. Lana could not accept "black and white" value systems.

On the Thinking (T)—Feeling (F) Scale: The only scale on which both had the same preference. Their preference for Feeling was evident in the efforts of both to express their personal values and reactions to the situation. This commonality was underscored and much validation given for the efforts and openness both displayed in dealing with the conflict. Also underscored was the common motivation to enhance the friendship, a "Feeling" value of both.

On the Judgment (J)—Perception (P) Scale: Mary's perference for Judgment was reflected by her need for more structure and security. She wanted to know in advance when Lana brought a boyfriend to the room. She wanted the use of the room (sleeping, socializing, etc.) to be more planned out and to feel as if she were in control of these issues. Lana, on the other hand, with a perference for Perception, disliked setting down or agreeing to a specific plan for the room. She preferred spontaneous activity and variety from day to day. Furthermore, she tended to be less orderly in housekeeping than Mary. Finally, Lana rarely saw issues as "black and white" and could not understand Mary's definite positions on issues such as dating.

From this discussion, Mary and Lana participated in clarifying some of their needs in relation to the living situation:

Mary's needs—sanctuary, privacy, security, a "good" image among peers.

Lana's needs—freedom, individuality and non-conformity, understanding and acceptance.

Mary and Lana now were able to move beyond the stuck point of "I can't understand why you do this" to a clear understanding that there were strong individual differences in style and values. Mary might not be able to grasp Lana's perspective, but she could accept the differences described by the MBTI. Lana gained a new appreciation for Mary's difficulty in living with Lana's way of doing things.

Moving from insight to action, each was first asked to restate what she saw as the basic differences in style, values, and needs. Each gave the other feedback on the accuracy of these statements. Their perspectives had become more objective, less personalized, and less emotional. With this more objective viewpoint they were better able to see actions that could be taken.

I then confronted them with a decision point. There were definite personality differences which had been and could continue to be a source of conflict. These differences had nothing to do with the qualities of each as a person. They could choose to find new roommates, or they chould choose to work on these differences. In the latter case, the basic differences could provide excitement and a growth experience for both. This could be a complementary relationship, where each could benefit from the strengths of the other (e.g., Mary could provide a sense of stability; Lana could introduce new experiences).

Lana and Mary chose to remain roommates because they both valued the friendship and felt confident in their abilities to communicate with each other. With coaching, they then worked through some basic issues of daily living, compromising to meet each other's needs. Examples of some of the compromises and ground rules established were:

— Lana would check with Mary before bringing young men to the room.
— Mary would not try to "preach" to Lana about her dating behaviors.
— Lana would find other locations for socializing besides their room.

None of these compromises was forced but were carefully thought through and volunteered by Mary and Lana. This communication model for specifying behaviors, times, and conditions is similar to that utilized in marriage/couples counseling.

Finally, they were asked to return in several weeks to let me know how things were going. At that follow-up and again three months later, they reported reduced tension and increased satisfaction with each other as roommates. They were able to view themselves and their differences with good humor.

Jeri - ISTJ
Resistance to Change

Jeri's process was much like Jesse's (ISFJ). In my practice, ISTJ dynamics are frequently similar clinically to those of ISFJ's. Jeri's case will illustrate several additional aspects of this related Type. Jeri came to see me because of stress and worries about not getting "all A's" her first term in college. She felt "tight" and anxious with freqent "tension headaches". She had rigidly set the "all A" standard for herself and was now angry with the system (teachers, methods of evaluation) and herself for not meeting this standard. Jeri was an extreme perfectionist in all areas of her life— appearance, eating behaviors, friendships, and general coping methods. For example, her naturally curly hair was a constant frustration to her since she couldn't "control" it. Her method of coping was to pomade her hair and braid it tighly. In her friend- ships she had rigid expectations of how her girlfriends **should** act, when they **should** call, etc.

Although she expressed unhappiness at her stress level, she was unwilling to examine her underlying assumptions, standards, and coping style. What she wanted from me was a formula for success to achieve her original goal of all A's. The counseling process was described to her as one of working together to sort out problems and find alternatives. I was not there to make her decisions or tell her what to do. Jeri was obsessive-compulsive, strongly defended, and reluctant to question or modify any of these defenses. ENFP therapists often have a tendency to push for change. However, I saw that even a gentle nudge caused her to hold on even more tightly to established beliefs and coping patterns.

Starting where she was, or conceptually geting into her current life space, became essential to any counseling progress. This meant trying to see the world through her ISTJ eyes and to use her "language" (vocabulary meaningful to her). Together we examined her study techniques. Her approach was rigid and concrete. She overstudied by reading material over and over, trying to memorize everything. Although this approach had worked in high school, it unfortunately did not work well with abstract, college level course material, which requires a higher level of learning (analysis and synthesis). She had difficulty particularly with essay tests and term papers. We discussed linear and global learning styles in terms of her Sensing preference. Her S influenced her to learn in a linear, sequential, step-by-step way; many of her courses necessitated global, non-sequential, concept-linking learning. Suggestions were made for new study approaches, and referral was made to the study skills laboratory. Jeri was reluctant to let go of her old ways to try new approaches. She believed that "more of the same" or "just working harder" would produce the A's. She was, therefore, not very receptive to help from the skills center.

Discussion of her MBTI results (from freshman orientation testing) was limited to the above issues of learning style because of her defensiveness. She was secretive and would have felt the Indicator was intrusive if I had elaborated her results at this point.

Counseling goals with Jeri were limited. She achieved some relief from her stress and frustration by being able to ventilate feelings and receive support, but she was not ready to modify her approach. She continued to insist on results (A's) and remained frustrated with the "system" and herself. Her tension headaches continued despite several sessions devoted to stress reduction through exercise and muscle relaxation. She decided that all her problems were physical. Consequently she persuaded her family doctor to write a prescription for Valium. Jeri then informed me that she felt counseling was no longer necessary since her family doctor was now "treating" her.

Her response was consistent with her early perception of her problem and of what counseling should be ("just give me the solution"). While conveying respect for her right to choose Valium as a way to control stress, I urged her to consider further counseling with me or someone not affiliated with the college. I voiced my personal concern that she look for other ways to deal with stress and my willingness to work with her in the future. In the last session we explored the possibility of Jeri taking time off from school. The evaluation process of school fed her obsessive preoccupations. Another environment, other than school, might allow her to grow and loosen her defenses. Jeri did, in fact, withdraw from school at the end of her freshman year, to work for a while. There was no way to know whether she sought further counseling after leaving.

Although her behavior was much more exaggerated than that of other ISTJ's I've observed clinically, Jeri shared several similar characteristics: a preference for concrete, structured outcomes in counseling (such as a pill) and discomfort with probing inner motivations and feelings. Mature ISTJ's, who are in the process of developing their third and fourth functions (F and N respectively), would be more amenable to insight or growth therapy. Perhaps a counselor close in Type to Jeri would have been more helpful. Jung talked about the benefits of pairing therapist and client of similar Types to lessen the gap in behavioral modeling.

Wendel - INTJ
In Pursuit of Utopia

Wendel came to see me in spring of his freshman year in college, because he felt unmotivated about school and lacked career direction. Interviewing revealed strong interests in nutrition, the outdoors, and athletics. His MBTI showed preference for INTJ. His Type tempered **how** he expressed these interests. For example, his interest in nutrition was directed to precise, scientific knowledge (NT) that would link what one ate with physical fitness. The outdoors, to Wendel, was a political battleground; his idealism about nature challenged the pollution and misuse of the land by modern technology (NTJ). His involvement in athletics was in terms of individual mastery (NT); desire for mastery was intense. He set extremely high standards of performance for himself and for his environment (NT, especially INTJ). No element of his surrounding environment met these standards. Furthermore, he was disappointed in himself for not meeting his standards (grades, athletic achievement, etc.). Wendel had a lot of "shoulds" about his academic performance and his behavior in general.

Many of the young INTJ's I have known are as intense and self-critical as Wendel. They are preoccupied with principles and mastery and often frustrated at not finding a clear, organized channel in which to direct themselves. Even in mid-life some of these frustrations may still exist.

His freshman MBTI results were discussed in relation to these personal characteristics, to career possibilities, and to academic adjustments. Wendel used his auxiliary function, Thinking, to deal with the world in a somewhat harsh and absolute manner. He was encouraged through counseling to view himself and others in a more gentle fashion. One way to accomplish this was to facilitate the development and use of his dominant Intuition. If Wendel could take a broader look at the many possibilities and dynamics in a given situation and in himself, he might be less absolute. He was challenged to look for patterns, motivations, and needs within himself and others. Viewing the world and himself with Intuition was new and exciting and seemed to free up some energy to deal

47

with school. One of the factors in his lack of motivation was his harsh internal "critic" who never encouraged. Wendel was helped to understand these internal dynamics and to work on being less critical. He could channel his T in more productive ways such as analyzing information and ideas.

Another aspect of his unmotivated attitude was the lack of a career goal. Several career areas were suggested, related to his interests, abilities, and Type. Some of these were: nutritional research, environmental studies/engineering, urban planning, natural resources management and forestry, biological/physical fitness research. Wendel's investigative NT was challenged to learn more about these career areas through reading, interviewing profess- ssionals in the field, a summer job, and possibly by volunteering in one of these fields. He planned to return in fall for follow-up counseling.

Wendel did return in fall, still feeling frustrated with himself, the people around him, and the college in general. He wanted to retake the MBTI and take the Strong-Campbell Interest Inventory (SCII). He also wanted to discuss transferring to a larger school with more of a vocational emphasis. Retesting confirmed the INTJ preferences. The SCII was not helpful because he marked so many responses "dislike" that results on all scales were "average" or below. Interests previously explored in our counseling sessions led him to choose forestry management as a tentative major. His MBTI Type could certainly find expression and satisfaction in that field. Wendel planned to transfer to a large state university offering this major but first wanted to spend some time traveling, camping, and working before returning to school.

Before Wendel left at the end of the term, we spent several more sessions working through his frustrations and continued self-criti- cism. Gestalt approaches were helpful in such areas as getting his discouraged self to confront his critical "top-dog" self through an "experimental" dialogue.

Several years later Wendel visited me and brought me up to date on what he had been doing. He had had several odd jobs to make money between outdoor expeditions. He was fiercely insistent on financial independence from his parents and lived a frugal, spartan lifestyle to achieve this independence. He had tried the state uni- versity but felt that the programs in forestry and environmental studies were "compromised" and not consistent with his ideals for the environment. His new goal was to look "outside the system" (outside academic conventional structures). He was interested in utopian societies and self-supporting communities that existed in harmony with the land. As Wendel talked, he conveyed strong conviction and determination to research these utopian societies and form one himself if he couldn't locate one already established. He had come to realize that his family and most others could not understand his "vision" and had accepted this. Although this visit was not a counseling session, I did remind him about Type theory—that he might need to temper his inner visions with outer reality, talk over his ideas and perceptions with respected individuals, and be realistic in what he expected from himself, others, and the environment.

Wendel was more comfortable with himself and was no longer as restless and frustrated as in his student days. He had a sense of direction and an awareness of the motivators, values, and preferences which shaped his choices. Wendel stated that learning about the MBTI had been a significant event in his growth. The insight about himself and validation of that self had much impact. He acknowledged the possibility that he might not succeed on this new path, but by following the path he would learn a great deal about himself and the world. He felt compelled to proceed in this individualistic, non-institutional way. Wendel specualted that perhaps someday he would return to academics to teach or research utopian societies and related issues.

In summary, the MBTI was quite helpful to Wendel in affirming his strengths, his uniqueness, and his need to do things differently from many fellow students. He was able to view his preferences with some humor and not take himself as seriously. Although he had a strong need to live by severe, ascetic standards and a sense of justice, he had discovered that if he carried this style "too far" (his words), he just frustrated and depressed himself. Instead, he channeled his IN into investigative efforts and new possibilities and as an NT "visionary" conceptualized and evaluated systems (communities, institutions). Finally, his strong J caused him to plan, structure, and persist.

INTROVERTED THINKING
with Intuition
INTP
T
N
S
F

Lorraine - INTP
The Need for Personal Space

When Lorraine arrived in my office immediately following referral by her academic advisor, she was in "overload". Lorraine felt as if she would "burst" but didn't undertand the origins of this feeling. She was very self-conscious about being in my office and about self-disclosing to someone she vaguely knew. Lorraine was a very private person who believed in solving problems carefully and thoroughly by herself.

Lorraine was a bright student who was not doing her work and was so far behind that she was now paralyzed about "catching up". In the accepting atmosphere of the counseling session, she was able to express tears of frustration and anger with "the system". The system of awarding financial aid was "unfair" in her eyes, penalizing her hard-working parents and expecting them to make "heavy sacrifices". She felt guilty about being in school when her parents were making financial sacrifices. She worried much about her parents, their growing old, and her alienation from them.

Concerns about her family led to exploration of her relationships with them. She expressed remorse that she had treated them so indifferently in high school and now realized how estranged she was from them. Lorraine thought she might transfer to a college closer to home so she could build a new relationship with her parents. We also explored the possibility of her doing this relationship building over summer vacation. Part of this session focused on **how** she could develop better communications with her parents. Her natural style was to be brief and assume people knew what she meant or felt, especially characteristic of INT's. We worked on improving her skills to be more self-disclosing and verbally responsive, focusing on anticipated situations with her parents.

Through counseling, Lorraine also became aware that she was grieving over the loss of her personal space. Before coming to college, she had her own room and now had a roommate. Previously she had a car in which she could also "escape" when she needed privacy. Now she saw herself as "trapped" on campus without a car. She had come to resent people around her and felt alienated.

A major intervention was explicit confirmation of her need for personal space as indicated by her MBTI Type. Earlier in the year, we had reviewed her MBTI results, as part of a freshman testing program. As an INTP (particularly the I), she needed time for herself every day and a place to be alone. We brainstormed private places she could go and how she could carve out quiet time from her schedule. Lorraine needed to give herself permission to take this time, since she felt guilty about not studying harder (when her parents were sacrificing financially). She decided to drop one course to reduce the pressure and free-up more time. We also discussed her need to become more aware of feelings as they developed, instead of waiting until these feelings reached eruptive proportions. The quiet time was suggested as a good time to "go inside" and notice how she was feeling about herself and others. This suggestion was presented in a logical, mater-of-fact way with a systems/efficiency rationale that appealed to her Thinking preference.

To find necessary order in her world, Lorraine needed to introvert, since her dominant function was introverted Thinking. Just making time to introvert and to use her T for evaluating her activities and current situation could help Lorraine stablize. She also needed to be aware of the fact that Feeling was her weakest function. By observing behavior of Feeling Types, she could increase her awareness of F so she could begin to recognize and develop it in herself.

She was encouraged to return for additional counseling to help her keep on track with her school work. I shared with her that many students with P preference, especially IP's fall into a procrastination pattern because of their preference for doing things at the last minute and not structuring their time. Through counseling these students learn techniques to reduce procrastination. In my college practice, INTP's seem to have the most difficulty of all the 16 Types (followed by the INFP's) with procrastination on written papers. Many of them have described their process as needing to think or "stew" on ideas internally for a long time, feeling as if they never have enough information to get started, being perfectionistic about the first sentences written down and the paper in general, and subsequently becoming more and more overwhelmed by the task and the little remaining time.

Lorraine came for only two sessions. Her emotional crisis had past. It had been difficult for her to open up to a stranger, but her high level of stress had propelled her to do so. Now that the anxiety was reduced, she did not wish to continue the counseling process. She had a high need to operate independently but knew I was there as a resource. The MBTI validated her need for personal space and also her strengths as an individual (her creativity, curiosity, patience, and interest in theory, etc.). She was more motivated to do her academic work, having replenished her emotional/spiritual self with some private time. Energy tied up in feeling guilty about her parents had been released through counseling and was now directed towards schoolwork. She was eager to spend time with her family and practice her new communications skills. At the end of the academic year, she transferred to a college closer to home. The counseling process had acknowledged Lorraine's individualistic style and fierce need for independence, while supporting her and offering her coping tools.

Billie - ENTP
The Unfocused Entrepreneur

Like Lorraine, Billie sought counseling during emotional overload, but after emotional discharge and brief counseling was unwilling to continue the sessions. Billie was self-referred following an extremely emotional confrontation with her mother over her two failed courses and generally poor academic performance. Billie was the oldest child of her widowed mother. She felt a great deal of pressure to succeed because of her place in the family and came to college with high expectations for success. Her excellent high school grades had supported this expectation.

Billie appeared agitated, and her thought process was very scattered. She spoke rapidly and without focus. Using a Gestalt approach, she was directed to slow down and pay attention to body sensations and internal emotional impressions. She was asked to report in detail on everything she was experiencing in the "here and now". This task helped to "ground" and focus her. What emerged was an awareness of feeling like two people—a "superficial" self and a "true" self. Her superficial self was easily influenced by peers and was non-assertive in that regard; she lacked self-control, partied heavily, and was sexually active with many casual partners. Her "true" self was vulnerable and afraid of failing. This self wanted more self-control, assertive responsibility-taking, and academic and career direction.

Viewing her present college lifestyle, she expressed a desire to "turn over a new leaf", to work toward the goals of understanding herself and developing more self-control. The plan mutually formulated was to:

— join an assertiveness training group
— work with the learning center to develop organization and study skills
— learn about aspects of herself through the MBTI
— set realistic goals for herself, including career/academic goals
— work on improving communications with her mother

55

Billie proved to be a poor candidate for the assertiveness group. Her energy level was almost hyperactive and her attention span so short that she could not contribute appropriately. The other group members were distracted and confused by her. After one session she withdrew from the group and worked with me individually, though briefly, on assertiveness skills.

Billie began missing her individual appointments after a few sessions. She was difficult to keep focused in sessions, avoiding further discussion of feelings or self-exploration by telling disconnected stories. When gently confronted with her avoidance behavior, she denied the behavior and stated she felt as if she were back in control and "everything was going right". At this time she admitted to heavy partying, involving use of alcohol and drugs, but was evasive about specific use. She appeared to be flitting from one campus activity to the next, in "butterfly" fashion. This butterfly behavior is a frequent characteristic of EP's who have not developed their Judgment function. Billie did not seem to use her Thinking to evaluate appropriateness of behavior or consequences or to prioritize activities. For example, she did not evaluate the consequence of her alcohol use in relation to her grades. She also seemed reluctant at that time to work on developing this function through further counseling.

She was, however, interested in preliminary career exploration. The MBTI scales were discussed in terms of her strengths with application to career areas. Her interests, energy, and Type led to considering careers with outdoor and adventure aspects. She was particularly interested in environmental studies and oceanography. With ability, these careers can be satisfying to the NT's because of their usual liking for abstract theories, sciences, technology, and systems. However, Billie expressed great impatience about the time one must spend in the classroom to prepare for these careers.

To channel her restless energy and interests, Billie decided to work part-time. She had a series of entrepreneurial sales jobs—creating art designs on surfboards, selling solar energy devices, etc. These jobs held more interest and were a higher priority to her than her studies.

Billie followed a pattern similar to other male and female ENTP students I have counseled. The pattern involves academic problems in association with heavy drinking, partying, busying oneself with everything but the academics, and stronger interest in the "real" world than in college. Often these students feel strongly pulled to go out and have adventures, make their own money, achieve independence. They are more likely than many other Types to drop out of college temporarily or permanently to achieve these ends. These entrepreneurial ENTP's, so anxious for stimulation, often form their own businesses. I encourage those restless ENTP's who wish to complete a degree, to work, volunteer, or have some non-college activity while going to school. I also work with them to develop their Thinking function, so that they may focus and direct their Intuition and prioritize activities. Of course, as in Billie's case, clients may not be willing to continue counseling and focus on using their T.

Billie was not ready for in-depth counseling, although by the end of that academic year, she had reduced the number of her extracurricular activities and was somewhat more organized about her studies. She still chose to approach living in a highly adventurous, non-conforming, and independent manner. She wanted "to find out for myself". She withdrew at the end of that year and was unclear about whether she would work for a while or attend another college. Billie will probably seek counseling when the next crisis occurs.

Joy - ESFP
Spinning Her Wheels

Joy was self-referred halfway through her freshman year because she was behind in all her school work and felt as if she were "going crazy". Like the other EP's in this casebook, she displayed much agitation, dramatic gestures, and hysterical behavior.

Joy's relationships with her family and her boyfriend were her highest priorities. None of these relationships was satisfactory at the time she sought counseling. Consequently she could not concentrate on her studies. Her parents had divorced the previous year. She felt "in the middle" and had much unexpressed anger towards them. In the session she became aware of experiencing this anger as tension and shaking in her upper body. A Gestalt activity helped her to express this anger using her arms, pillows, and verbalizations to accompany her catharsis. Joy's boyfriend had been the stabilizing force in her life during the past few years but was now over 1000 miles away at another college. She felt a real loss of his support and felt the relationship was strained by the distance. Her way of coping was "spinning her wheels"; sitting staring at her books and worrying about these relationships, or avoiding work altogether by socializing with other friends. Joy also distracted herself by getting involved in many students' personal problems, trying to "solve" them.

As an ESFP, Joy sought high stimulation and action through the Sensing channel, her dominant function. She needed to introvert to access and to understand her feeling responses. Introverting in this way could cause a shift from amorphous awareness of a "block" of feelings to awareness of the discreet feelings within. Pounding and squeezing pillows to focus her attention through action, followed by quiet assessment of what was happening inside, were helpful to her.

As she began to understand her feelings and their origins, she began to move towards actions which would resolve these feelings. For example, her upper-class, status-conscious parents pressured her to choose a career with prestige, such as law. Joy, on the other hand, was not interested in long-term education. She was interested in working with children as a career and as a mother. Yet, she had not asserted this with her parents; she had complied with their academic plans for her while resenting them. She had tried "not to rock the boat" during this time of marital conflict. Consequently Joy rebelled periodically by not studying or by acting out through petty conflict with her parents. Joy's desired actions were to learn to be more assertive with her parents, to avoid "being in the middle" with them, to tell them about her interests in working with children, and to make career plans consistent with her needs.

In the second session, another counseling goal was mutually established: to help her achieve some personal balance by learning to use her Thinking function. For example, her Thinking function was engaged to analyze the chain of events and behaviors which precipitated a conflict with parents. We examined links in the chain that could be broken to interrupt the fight sequence, such as: What were the cues that "hooked" her into fighting?; How could she respond differently?; etc. Joy responded well to this approach to family conflict and to other Thinking interventions such as applying Ellis' Rational Emotive Therapy to understand how her negative thinking influenced her emotional responses. She was ready to find a "more adult" way to respond to highly charged situations. These Thinking approaches had a calming or balancing effect.

The MBTI was utilized to help her understand her present coping style and also to explore possible career directions. Although I had incorporated knowledge of Joy's MBTI into my counseling approach with her, MBTI concepts were not introduced until several sessions were devoted to her affective state. Earlier interpretations of her results would have been inappropriate because of her emotional state and confusion. Her interests in working with children and in coaching athletics and recreational groups were validated. I have found that young ESFP's often are heavily involved in team sports in high school and even in the lower grades. They are group-oriented and love playful action. They also tend to like and do well in coaching because of sensitivity to others' responses and their ability to generate enthusiasm. These characteristics, of course, may apply in child development careers as well. Joy's flexibility (P) and attention to practicalities (S) were also cited as useful in these careers. She felt more positively about herself, and decided to major in elementary education or early child development. She realized she would have to assert these plans with her parents to achieve her goals but also realized her former way of dealing with them was non-productive and destructive. Joy made the decision to transfer to a school with her chosen academic major which was also closer to her boyfriend.

Before she left, we did additional work on developing awareness or discreet feelings (as opposed to hysterical responses) and ways of expressing these feelings. She was encouraged to have an outlet through daily physical activity. Joy, like many ESP's, relied heavily on external controls, such as a boyfriend or peers, to shape her behavior. She regularly found herself **reacting** to these external factors with little use of any internal self-control mechanism. We explored ways she could develop internal control, using her evaluative or judging function, F. The Judgment function was related to time management and setting priorities based on **her** needs, not on those of her friends.

Joy was motivated to work in counseling because her relationships were very important. It was also easy to develop rapport with her. She was able to succeed academically once she achieved a level of self-understanding. She ended counseling when she transferred. Joy left with a better sense of self, more confidence in her ability to interact with her parents as an adult, and anticipation of a meaningful career direction.

James - ISTP
Freshman Panic

"Feeling is the least manageable process for an ISTP. If too suppressed, it can build up pressure and explode in most inappropriate ways." James' reactions during the first week of college are accurately described by this quote from CAPT's interpretive printout. He was referred to me by campus police following an outburst of irrational and potentially suicidal behavior. James had had too much to drink, become morose and confused, felt alienated, panicked, and had begun acting bizarrely. He expressed thoughts of ending his life.

At first James was quite embarrassed by the referral for counseling and for all the attention he had attracted. He was encouraged to express underlying feelings, concerns, and tensions which had led to this acting out. James' predominant feeling was one of alienation, saying that the people at college were not "real", and therefore he couldn't relate to them. He missed his girlfriend back home; she had been a source of security and support. James' parents were both high achievers who expected great things from their son. James was not sure that college was for him. In fact, he had made a feeble suicidal gesture while going through the college application process the year before. It appeared that not only was he experiencing the loss of his previous support system but also that he felt pressured by expectations to succeed academically and socially.

In an intensive, two hour session, he ventilated these feelings. Although reluctant to do so at first, his anxiety propelled him to disclose. Talking appeared to bring relief and a lightening of affect. He expressed appreciation for the "meaningful contact" with me, his first "real" contact at college, according to him. This behavior of disclosing feelings was new to James. The importance of expression was explained to him in rational terms. By attending to feelings as they occurred, James could avoid explosive crises which caught him off balance.

Frequently ITP's, in whom Feeling is the least preferred function, are startled or even frightened by sudden bursts of emotion which seem to come from "nowhere". Their lack of orientation toward processing feelings causes emotions to have an unknown or almost mysterious quality. A normal situation which does not generate

63

intense emotional response can be handled with Thinking; this function can identify and label the response in an objective fashion. Intense responses, however, cannot easily be managed in the same analytical labelling style. Thus, when this Thinking approach fails to manage strong feelings, as in James' situation, panic may occur because of this failure of the familar coping mechanism. A vicious cycle can emerge: strong emotional response, attempt to handle through Thinking objectively, continued strong emotion, further panic at lack of control, and bewilderment. The cycle can be broken, first, by supporting expression of strong feelings in a safe, controlled environment. Second, following catharsis, ITP clients can be helped to understand their internal process and to learn other ways of handling feelings. Emotions can be demystified so that they will be less intimidating.

After James' affect shifted from an explosive to a stabliized state, we focused on the process of adjustment to college, particularly the social aspects. **How** did he go about making contact with his peers? We discussed concrete behaviors that he could try; this concrete approach appealed to his Sensing. He admitted to "posing" and "playing games" and therefore was challenged to be more real himself. The importance of self-disclosure and trust in developing friendships was stressed. I suggested he also avoid drinking until he felt more stabilized on campus, since his drinking could precipitate another outburst or panic. I determined that James was not suicidal. He agreed to contact me immediately if he entertained further suicidal thoughts.

Finally, James was encouraged to continue counseling to practice attending to his feelings and to assure adjustment to college. James was reluctant to continue counseling, since he perceived his problem as immediate and transitory. I expressed respect for his decision but left the door open for further sessions and suggested he at least consider me a "safety valve" for expressing feelings. He said he felt relieved to know he was not alone. Like many other ISP's I have worked with, James' tendency was to seek brief counseling for a crisis only. We had not discussed his MBTI results in this single crisis intervention session but I encouraged him to return when he was ready to explore the MBTI in relation to academic work and career possibilities.

Later in the year, James returned for consultation. He brought a friend with him. Both were seeking advice on how to help a mutual friend with a serious drinking problem. He also referred several other friends for counseling during the year. He appeared to view me as a resource and support. Yet he did not feel a need for growth or insight counseling. James said he now had a close network of friends, was handling the academic work successfully, and was pleased with his adjustment to college. Seeing him around campus, he appeared cheerful and socially involved.

Dave - ESTP
Reluctant Student

Like James, Dave was referred for potentially suicidal behavior during a heavy drinking episode. He was embarrassed to have made "such a display" of his feelings and said he didn't feel as if he "fit in" at the college.

His family was far away, and he was having trouble initiating new friendships. In addition, Dave had recently received his first grades; two unsatisfactories at mid-term of his first semester. He was discouraged but not suicidal. He had no organized approach for studying. The several ensuing counseling sessions focused on social and academic adjustment.

One session was devoted to interpretation of his MBTI results. During discussion of ESTP's preferences for immediacy, action, and direct Sensing experience, Dave admitted that he really did not want to be in college. His parents had pressured him with their expectations that he should become a "professional". Dave wanted to become a flight attendant instead of going to college. He was resentful and angry, especially towards his father, but had never expressed his feelings and desires to his parents. Instead his solution was to "go around" his parents, satisfying their basic demands so that he could reap material benefits from them. He was reluctant to "rock the boat" because financial support might be cut off. Material comforts were a high priority to him.

We rehearsed how he might assertively communicate to his parents his feelings about college and a career without causing intense conflict. Since Dave saw no virtue in communicating feelings, practical reasons for expression were put forth, appealing to his Sensing preference; e.g. unexpressed resentment could cause depression or decrease his ability to function at school and in general. Furthermore, his parents were not mind readers. Dave could see how our counseling sessions had brought some emotional relief so that he was no longer as overwhelmed and discouraged.

The MBTI indicated preferences which could be suited to an airline career as pilot, operations officer, or possibly flight attendant. More F's than T's would be expected in this latter occupation because of required sensitivity to passenger needs. SF's are more likely to seek service jobs. ESTP's are "trouble shooters", often good at sizing up the needs of the moment and operating quickly with common sense and objectivity. These strengths are helpful in unpredictable and changeable circumstances, such as in the travel industries. Of course, it was pointed out to Dave that other career areas could also utilize these strengths.

Often ESTP's have difficulty feeling motivated to do academic work unless they have well-formulated, practical goals. Distribution requirements, such as an introductory philosophy course, may seem meaningless and irrelevant to them. Like many other P's, they often are not organized in study habits. Therefore, in addition to exploring the meaning of college for Dave, I encouraged him to attend the Learning Skills Center to develop better study skills. I stressed that he would "enjoy" college more with these acquired skills (and enjoyment is a strong motivator for most ESTP's).

Dave's concerns for social adjustment were first met with supportive statements about the typical adjustment patterns of most freshmen. Some examples of others' similar experiences and a simple explanation of his developmental stage—transition to college—helped him to feel "normal" and not alone in his concerns. I was fairly direct and more informative than I might be working with an Intuitive client, because Dave's least developed function was N, and the pattern of his transition to college was not apparent to him. We examined available opportunities for developing new friends and getting involved. Since he had been socially successful in high school, he did not seem to need social skill building but rather just encouragement and reassurance.

After a few sessions, Dave had become more involved on campus and felt good about his new college friends. He was unwilling to be open with his parents as yet. He had decided "to stick it out" for his freshman year and they try to get a job with the airlines. He was encouraged to return for additional counseling as needed and to keep in touch, to let me know how he was doing. Dave remained in college and consulted with me periodically when he preceived himself as needing guidance in a specific situation. He was active in a fraternity, maintained a "C" average, but had not yet finalized his career plans.

Dave had been very self-conscious in initial counseling sessions, expressing concern that he had acted foolishly. Although he was motivated to resolve his anxieties about being in college, he did not wish to probe deeply into his own intrapsychic functioning. Like many ES's, he wanted to take quick action. The MBTI was a useful tool for many reasons but especially for discriminating whether Dave's reaction to college was purely parental rebellion or whether in part it was a reflection of his preferences.

Carmen - ISFP
Brief Counseling

Like many other ISFP's and the ISTP and ESTP cases presented earlier, Carmen was referred in crisis and terminated counseling as soon as the crisis was resolved. Carmen was referred to me by the college physician who had treated her for acute gastric distress. Carmen was emotionally overloaded. Her boyfriend had just been arrested for drug dealing and placed in an involuntary treatment program. Her parents had just separated, each taking one of the children and "splitting the family in half". Carmen felt as if she had lost her family, her home, her boyfriend and feared also losing her student status. She could not concentrate on studies and was already on academic probation.

I encouraged her to follow the physician's treatment plan for her gastric symptoms and to discuss her academic status with her faculty advisor. Then we focused on identification and expression of specific feelings related to the above life issues. She began to understand the nature of her stress reaction, physically and mentally. Carmen expressed relief at being heard and understood by someone; she had felt so alone in her crisis. Carmen needed a great deal of support and some point of stability in her currently chaotic life. Doing well academically so she could stay in school was thus important to her need for stability.

Carmen tended to focus on emotional issues over which she had no control. This focus increased her anxiety level. She also had been internalizing her anxieties which led to the gastric symptoms. Utilizing her preference for Sensing, I asked her to focus on issues she **could** do something about, practically speaking. Once she had ventilated feelings, she was ready for a problem solving mode. The drug treatment program would not allow her to contact her boyfriend; she thus felt helpless in regard to him. Carmen could dispel some of this helplessness by contacting the program director and learning more about his treatment. This small step gave her a sense of being more in control. She also needed to talk to both of her parents about not being "put in the middle" or not "having to

67

chose sides''. We role played several conversations with her parents in which she expressed her emotional need for both of them. She was encouraged also to allow herself to grieve over the loss of her home, and the process of grieving was supported as necessary in order to get on with living.

The MBTI suggested ways I could utilize Carmen's strengths to cope with her crisis. Her auxiliary Sensing seemed well-developed for dealing with the external world. With encouragement she was able to use her Sensing to find practical solutions and take each moment as it came. Carmen needed validation of her dominant Feeling. The validation of her Feeling function had a calming, stablizing effect.

In the next session we further explored her academic situation and discussed the MBTI in this regard. Her preferences for ISFP were related to learning style and study habits. We discussed some methods to become more organized, since, like many other ISFP's, she was somewhat of a "free spirit" about studying. She was referred to a study techniques workshop and to tutors. We explored the potential "traps" for her Type that could prevent her from sticking to her study plan. For example, her intense internalized feelings needed to be discharged or she would not be able to concentrate on schoolwork. Her preference for P could cause her to rebel against too rigid a schedule, especially if she didn't build in some social, fun rewards (SFP) for completing parts of her schedule. She was motivated to improve her studying because completing school would please her family and give her status. However school was **not** important to her at that time for intellectual growth, per se. These motivators were strong enough to influence her to work with her advisor and tutors to improve her grades.

Her advisor and a college administrator served as parental figures who could regularly check on her progress. These professionals were extrenal stimuli for her to become more responsible and organized. Carmen was encouraged to touch base with me periodically as an "anchor" or support. She reported better communications with her parents, understanding and acceptance of her boyfriends's situation, improvement of her physical condition, and a calmer state in general. Carmen worked hard enough to remove herself from academic probation and graduated with the rest of her class.

Richard - ESFJ
The Need to Please

Richard, age 19, was self-referred with many questions about interpersonal relationships. He was unhappy with his friendships and felt he was being "used" by his friends. He said he was always doing favors and giving to other materially and emotionally. Yet he felt his friends rarely reciprocated. Richard assumed that friends would "know" that he needed the same kinds of attention and caring he gave to them. His generosity led to criticism from his parents for spending too much money on his friends. Observing his interactions, his pattern was to interact with effusive warmth, often offering gifts or favors, and then to feel hurt and resentful when he was not "appreciated".

We briefly discussed the relevance of his MBTI results to his interactions. Since his dominant function was Feeling, harmony and approval were crucial. Richard had difficulty saying no to friends' requests, as many strong Feeling Types do. Also as an SJ, especially SFJ, he needed expressions of appreciation from friends for "the little things" he did for them. From our discussion, Richard learned that the other 15 MBTI Types had different values and ways of interacting. Therefore, Richard could not assume that his friends could "know" what he needed from them, or that they even valued the same things. This insight was particularly helpful to him, although he regretted having to adjust his thinking in this matter (others "**should** feel the same way").

Richard was the youngest of four and had always played the harmonizer and pleaser role in his family. His mother could always count on him to run errands when the other children refused. His parents disapproved of his pursuing an academic major in the performing arts. Since he was concerned about pleasing his parents, his interest in the performing arts created a conflict.

Much of our work centered on challenging his irrational thinking that he "must please everybody". Albert Ellis' Rational Emotive Therapy constructs were used to help him examine his thoughts and attitudes about people and himself. Rational Therapy demands use of the Thinking function in systematically analyzing and objectively evaluating thoughts/self-talk in relation to the actual facts and events. This therapeutic approach has been particularly helpful with Feeling Types who need to achieve some balance by developing the Thinking function. This approach must be introduced gently to F's, however, after rapport is established. Otherwise Feeling clients may reject the therapist and this therapeutic approach as "cold", "insensitive" and "irrelevant" to them.

Assertiveness training was also introduced so that he would not continue to feel used. Techniques were taught and practiced on how to say no and how to ask for what he needed from his friends. Richard responded very positively to this approach, returning to report new successes in relating to his friends. He needed much encouragement and support for trying these new behaviors, because he had such strong self-talk that he must be "nice" to everyone. The structured assertiveness techniques appealed to his SJ preferences for structure and practical suggestions. Assertiveness training also stimulates functioning of the Thinking function, since the client must anwer the question, "What are my personal right here?" and analyze behavioral choices and consequences.

Another practical intervention was to work on his breathing to interrupt anxiety reactions. When conflict emerged in a relationship, he began to breathe shallowly, talk faster, get more and more flustered and became unable to communicate assertively. This breathing response to anxiety could be observed during counseling. His experience with voice lessons had taught him a method of deep breathing which he could employ to interrupt his anxiety cycle. He was instructed to monitor his rate of speech, breathing, and feelings and to use breathing to calm himself. Because this suggestion took advantage of his natural preference for Sensing, he was enthusiastic and successful with this technique.

Richard responded well to counseling because of his motivation to change his relationships and because of the rapport developed in the counseling sessions. The MBTI suggested interventions that would assist in his Type development and was helpful to Richard in understanding individual differences. Counseling sessions spanned most of one school year on an irregular schedule. After termination of the counseling relationship, Richard came by periodically to chat briefly and let me know that things were going well for him. He continued with his theater major and established a more satisfying, adult relationship with his family.

Roger - ESTJ
Discomfort with the Unknown

Although I had known Roger as a student leader for four years and consulted with him about student organizations, he had never sought counseling until early spring of his senior year. Roger had always been extremely decisive and organized but suddenly found himself in an indecisive, complex situation. He expressed anxiety about this state of "vagueness" and requested the MBTI to help him in his future planning.

Roger scored as a well-defined ESTJ. He had questions about whether to go to law school or get an MBA. Should he go right on to graduate school or work for a while? Should he choose a geographical area close to family, or just take the best opportunity? Although most seniors experience anxiety over these kinds of questions, Roger's anxiety was intensified because of his natural preferences (ESJ) for resolving things quickly and simply. He was impatient with himself and concerned about making "the right" decision.

Values clarification and reflective listening/responding helped to clarify his present feelings and attitudes. Although Roger "tired" of school, he liked the "security" of the (graduate) school structure and the familiarity of the student role. Looking at the strengths of his Type and his past work/life experiences, we identified the kind of work he might find satisfying: day-to-day business management in a large, well-organized firm where he could have a great deal of people contact. We structured a job search plan, which appealed to his ESTJ approach of structure and practicality. The issue of security in relation to family was also explored. He was able to express his fear of making the major transition from school to the adult world. Roger was encouraged to weigh his need for family support versus taking a good job away from family. He was cautioned about the **potential** problem of ESTJ's (or ESFJ's) resolving things **too** quickly just to make a decision. With this self-awareness, he gave himself permission to postpone temporarily a decision about location so he could remain open to possibilities and awareness of his emotional needs.

71

Later in spring, Roger returned in a panic about what he termed "acute senioritis". He had been skipping classes and "even a test", which was totally uncharacteristic of him (and of ESTJ's in general). He didn't like this careless view of himself, and yet he couldn't get motivated. His anxieties about transition to the adult world were sabotaging his attempts to study. Continued exploration of these feelings allowed him to better focus on his studies. Unfortunately, his course load was so light that he could put off working, but then he couldn't get back into the work mode. In other words, he had lost his familiar work/study structure and felt generally lost. Roger also experienced guilt because his former conscientious, achieving ways had been replaced by "laziness".

My intervention was somewhat paradoxical. It gave Roger the opportunity to socialize and play more, which he wanted during his last months at school. Yet the intervention also gave him a structure in which to function. After examining his course load, I encouraged him to "allow" himself to study ONLY two days a week, no more (It was realistic for him to complete his specific work in that time period). On these two work days he was to work very hard and not play. The rest of the week he should not work but should socialize, job search, etc. Roger grinned broadly at this plan. He have never before been told **not** to study.

Upon follow-up after one week and again after three weeks, Roger was enjoying his schoolwork and his social life. He grinned and said, "It's working!". He continued to do well academically. We worked through a step-by-step decision making process for his post graduation plans. The MBTI in some ways gave him permission to fear the unknown and to desire security, since these are important issues for most STJ's. At the same time, his strengths for the job market were validated by the MBTI, increasing his confidence "to do the job" and to take on graduate school when he was ready. Following graduation he accepted a promising position in a management training program, close enough to his parents for weekend visits. Although ESTJ students are not as likely to seek ongoing, growth-oriented counseling, students like Roger are eager for short term, structured interventions that meet their immediate needs.

Mara - ENTJ
Developing Tact and Patience

Mara was referred by the college physician the second week of school because of nervousness and difficulty sleeping. Mara appeared to be struggling to hold herself together and was extremely tense. Home was far away. She was feeling the loss not only of her family but also of her psychiatrist with whom she had worked weekly for several years. The psychiatrist had been her only emotional "outlet"; she had not confided in family or peers. Suddenly she had no outlet and felt extremely tense. Talking gave her insight about the significance of this loss and brought an outburst of tears and subsequent relief. She had felt "embarrassed" to cry in front of her roommate and had invested a lot of energy in trying to cover-up her anxiety. Mara also put much pressure on herself to do well socially and academically in college.

Mara was encouraged to share feelings with her roommate, since expression of feelings prevented severe tension build-up. The rationale for expression of feelings needed to be couched in logical terms to appeal to her Thinking. It was also apparent that she had some difficulty in identifying emerging feelings and might not recognize these until they reached eruptive proportions. Feeling was her least-preferred function. One of our counseling goals was to help her identify feelings sooner and learn to express them. Feelings, it was explained, were "as real as facts" and must be dealt with.

Mara was encouraged to develop new friendship that could also be a support and outlet for her. She had difficuty forming friendships, however, because she "came on too strong" and often treated others with impatience. If a conflict arose, she tended to state her opinion tactlessly and alienate her friend. We spent several sessions on assertive, as opposed to aggressive, ways of handling conflict and of communicating in general.

Besides this important social outlet, she was encouraged to get regular physical activity to help with sleeping. I also taught her a relaxation exercise to use during study times and at bedtime.

Several weeks later she was pleased to report she was sleeping better and had followed my suggestions. She was sharing more with her roommate and found her to be surprisingly receptive and supportive. She also was more aware of how she communicated with others.

Later in the year, Mara came back to discuss academic majors in relation to her MBTI strengths as an ENTJ. She expressed an interest in psychology and in marketing. Industrial psychology and marketing could be opportunities to channel ENTJ strengths: e.g., a natural desire to lead; an interest in creating, analyzing, and changing systems; a tendency towards long-range planning and structuring; impersonal objectivity; a desire for innovation and creativity; a liking for intellectual challenge and complexity. Mara was encouraged to sample courses in these areas and also plan some "real world" experiences in these areas, such as internships.

Mara saw me periodically whenever she became frustrated with her social situation. She tended to attach herself to a boyfriend and depend on this one individual for her intimacy needs. This was easier for her than establishing and maintaining several other friendships, especially with women. She did have many superficial friendships. When the boyfriend relationship was in trouble, she became anxious. After several boyfriends and several crises, I confronted her about this pattern. Mara began to work more deliberately towards a broader social base. She continued to battle with her impatience towards others and herself. Her NT desire for mastery, coupled with her EJ action/completion preferences contributed greatly to this impatience. She was not naturally empathic and had to work to become more sensitive to others' responses. She was motivated to work at this because of her emotional needs and career ambitions, where she saw these skills as important. Mara had made a reasonable adjustment during her first year in college. Mara did not contact me for further counseling. When seen later around campus, she seemed to be functioning well and graduated with a major in psychology.

Tom - ENFJ
Guilt and Punishment

Tom was referred by his academic advisor because he seemed to be "drifting" in college, when by now, as a junior, he should have had more direction. Tom was interested in learning his MBTI results and how these might apply to several career considerations. We discussed options such as majoring in business, taking a position in sales, going to law school or graduate school immediately following his B.A. degree. We examined these options in light of his preferences for ENFJ. His "people" skills and interest in communicating and working with groups could be applied to many business settings. His Extraverted energy and preferences for structure could be valuable in many of these career areas. Some cautions about law were discussed since he had a strong preference for Feeling. A majority of attorneys are Thinking Types. This fact was not presented as a deterrent to the selection of law as a career, but rather as an opportunity for him to examine his own motives and interests in law. Also, he was encouraged to learn more about this field in terms of day-to-day functioning.

I encouraged him to continue with more sessions on career planning, since discussion of the MBTI was only a start. I sensed a reluctance on his part to continue counseling, and again his word "drifting" seemed to fit even in the counseling process.

I saw Tom a few months later when he was referred again, this time by the college physician after an episode of heavy drinking in which he seriously injured himself. Tom said he was relieved to be referred to me again and had been thinking of coming back to talk to me about personal issues. The drinking incident was a culmination of several others that year. This episode, however, had severely frightened him with his "self-destructive tendencies". Tom felt as if he were out-of-control about his drinking, his impulsive behavior, and his study habits. His impulse at that moment was to run, to get away from the peer pressure to party, so he could "sort things out". I suggested he first get some food and rest and think about the questions he needed to ask himself. Then I wanted him to return the next morning, and we would explore the wisdom of his leaving school at that time. I also took a drinking history and determined (assuming he was truthful) that he was not alcoholic. The alcohol use at this point seemed symtomatic of some underlying emotional problem.

The following morning Tom returned in much better physical condition with a clearer mind. We began to explore his lack of motivation at school, self-destructive impulses, and underlying depression. He was suffering from a loss of self-esteem. In high school he had been the high achieving "good" student, whereas now he was behaving "irresponsibly". He judged himself harshly and did not like himself.

I discovered in the counseling process that his father had died a year ago that month, but that Tom's grieving had been attenuated. At the time of his fathers's death, Tom had allowed himself a brief emotional outburst but then had "run away" from the family's grieving and returned to school. The feelings about his father, which he had shelved, were now reemerging on the anniversary of his death. His mother had been highly emotional during his father's illness and especially after his death. Tom also was emotional and felt overloaded by his mother's desire to lean on him as the only son. He needed to lean, too, but found no one to support him. So he had "escaped" to school. Yet he felt guilty and bad for "abandoning" his family.

Tom had another issue in regard to his father. He discovered in counseling that he harbored anger and resentment towards his father for never having been there for him when Tom was a child. His father had been in a business requiring a great deal of travel. In order to finish grieving and relieve his depression, Tom needed to express these feelings toward his father. Tom was able to do this by imagining his father present in the counseling session and speaking to him.

I then asked Tom what he wished to do about his strained relationship with his mother. Tom realized that to feel better about himself he needed to "make things right" with his mother. We then role-played what he needed to say to his mother. He looked forward to the coming summer vacation when he could return home and repair family relationships.

Tom was given acceptance and respect for feelings towards his family. He was helped to express and clarify powerful emotions he had tried to suppress but which had affected his ability to function. He was guided towards understanding the grieving process and thus gained insight about his responses to his father's death.

I challenged Tom, then, to use his Intuition and look at the pattern of his school behavior in light of these feelings we had uncovered. Tom's auxiliary function was fairly well-developed.

With some encouragement to go inside (to Introvert) and take the time to access this function, he arrived at some insights. He saw that his heavy drinking and related behaviors were a way to punish himself and confirm his "badness" in relation to his family. He expressed surprise at how these feelings, avoided for so long, had affected his behaviors and sense of self. He was now ready to "forgive" himself for running from his family. As an ENFJ, he had set very high expectations for himself about being a "good" son, but was now ready to see himself as more human than super-human. He had done the best he could at the time. Now he was stronger and ready to give more to his family and to himself. We had no further counseling contact, although he knew "the door was always open". Tom graduated the following year.

Chapter V
OBSERVATIONS AND SUMMARY

Some patterns can be discerned from the 18 cases of the preceding chapter. However, it would be wrong to belabor similarities and differences or to make categorical statements, such as all those of a certain Type present certain behaviors. Certainly, as stated earlier, there are great variations within the 16 Types. Those who seek counseling may be different in some ways from others of the same Type who do not preceive a need for counseling. Readers are reminded again that many of these cases are **young** Types, who have for the most part not had time to develop their auxiliary, third, and fourth functions. We should expect these young Types to appear different in some ways from their older counterparts. In addition, by not representing each sex for all Types, some possible sex differences may have been overlooked. In my clinical work, though, I have found age and environment to be stronger factors than sex in variation within Types.

Readiness to work with the counselor/therapist and to experiment with using MBTI functions other than the favorite is a reoccurring theme in these 18 cases. The counselor may assess the need for function development in an immature Type with little balance, but the client must agree to this counseling goal and respond to interventions related to Type development for change to occur. Many of the cases presenting acute stress showed motivation to continue counseling only as long as the crisis was unresolved. Some were unwilling to try new coping skills that were not a function of their strongest preferences.

The number of sessions of counseling seemed most related to the T-F scale. F clients were more likely to stay in counseling for a longer length of time, regardless of their other preferences. Type similarity between counselor and client does not seem to be a factor in the number of counseling sessions. For example, the ISFJ was more dissimilar than the ENTP to my Type of ENFP yet had many more sessions. Although more cases would be needed to verify a pattern in the number of sessions related to the T-F scale, two possible explanations occur to me. One is that my personality and interaction style appeal more to F's than T's. Even more likely to be a factor, is that F Types generally seem to have a higher need for verbalizing emotional concerns and perhaps are quicker and more ready to identify their responses as such. F's may "enjoy" the counseling process more than T's. The T's as a whole may not trust the subjectivity they perceive to be inherent in the counseling process. T's may be unwilling to invest much time and money in counseling, which often has no quantifiable outcomes.

Certain issues and concerns seemed more common with certain Types. Dependency issues seemed to be associated more with the J preference than any other. J's often need more structure and security especially in making a major transition, such as going away to college and leaving familiar support structures behind. J's do not generally shift gears or adapt as quickly as the P's. The P's had more difficulties in organizing themselves, developing study habits, handling procrastination, staying motivated, and learning to set priorities. In relation to the latter, P's seemed frequently to have trouble using their judging function (T or F). The EP's among these cases tended toward unfocused, frantic, and sometimes hysterical behavior. The themes of alienation and poor social skills, whether the presenting problem or a secondary theme, seemed most present in the NT's, especially the INT's. The ENTP was the exception and behaved more like the ENFP in relation to socialization. Readers may find it interesting to compare some of these observations with their own clinical observations and to the literature on the subject. For this purpose, I've included a brief discussion of some of the findings in the literature in regard to Type as a factor in counselor-client relationships, preferred mode of therapy, and presenting problems. The following references to the research literature do not comprise a thorough literature review but are included to stimulate the reader to consider these issues and perhaps conduct research themselves.

Client Types in Counseling

Mendelsohn and Geller (1977) reported fewer SJ's and more N's and P's using a college counseling center. Carskadon (1979) in a research review also reported a higher frequency of N's and NP's, especially for males; he found clinicians more frequently with preferences for N and NF. In this same research review, Carskadon notes Arain's (1967) findings of no correlation between presenting problem and Type in a high school student sample. Jones and Sherman (1979) had many interesting observations about Type patterns in the case load of a college counseling center. Some of these were:

— the most frequent Type seeking career counseling was the INFP;
— ENFP's needed academic counseling, were more rebellious and less willing to conform, and had poor study habits;
— students with mild or middle scores on the T-F scale had problems making decisions.

Bisbee, Mullaly, and Osmond (1982) studying a population of psychiatric patients in hospitals and clinics, had the following observations:

— the I,S,F,J and ISFP were more prone to depression and schizophrenia;
— the ISFP's were the most frequent substance abusers;
— bipolar manic-depressives were more frequently FJ, ESFJ, ENTP; there were few ST's in this diagnostic category.

Of course, none of these citings is conclusive, since there are many variables at play in these samples. Larger and more randomized samples must be researched before any conclusions can be drawn. Furthermore, there is still the problem of **who** is doing the diagnosing; perhaps the diagnostician's Type may interfere with an objective diagnosis of patients/clients of different Types! That is a fascinating question in itself. For example, what is "normal" for an INTP will probably be very different from the "normal" of an ESFJ.

Client-Counselor Relationships

Thompson (1977) reported a study in which similarity and difference between client and therapist were compared to perceived counseling outcomes. Counselors and clients were given the MBTI after counseling was terminated and outcome evaluations completed. Although no significant relationship occurred for Type when measuring clients' perceptions of positive outcomes, there was a significant relationship between Type and counselors' perceptions of positive outcomes. Similarity on the E-I and J-P scales between counselor and client was associated with positive counseling outcomes, as perceived by the counselor. Differences on these scales had the opposite relationship.

Mendelsohn and Geller found that the more different the client and counselor, the fewer were the number of sessions. They did not find the duration of counseling to be related to Type, per se.

Therapies

Arain found that T's preferred cognitive therapists, while F's preferred affective therapists. In Carskadon's review, he cites several studies while Rationale Emotive Therapy decreased irrational thinking in F's but did not have the same impact on T's. It was suggested that RET provided balance for F's; this pattern is certainly present in the cases presented in Chapter IV.

Conclusions about Type
and the Counseling Relationship

It would seem, then, that client-counselor similarity might be naturally more conducive to productive therapy and/or longer duration of counseling. Van Franz tells of Jung matching patients he referred to therapists of similar Type, "with the same blind spots", because "if two idiots sit together and neither can think, they will get into such trouble that at least one of them will begin to think!" (p. 4). With similarity there may be less of a gap to bridge in personal style (language, perception, etc.) and in behavior modeled by the therapist. Thus in Jesse's case, the large gap between my natural expression of "playfulness" (as an ENFP) and Jesse's (ISFJ) may have made it harder for her to try new behaviors. The steps may have seemed to large, like "giant steps" instead of "baby steps", and the task may have seemed insurmountable to her at times.

Of course, there is much to be learned from working with very different Types, who frequently teach me more about my own "blind spots" and weaknesses than those that are very similar to me. Counselors should try to engage the client and establish rapport using the client's language, based on knowledge of client's Type. I've tried to illustrate this in some of the cases. Counselors must respect differences in preference and the accompanying differences in values and attitudes. Certainly, counselors can be more effective with any Type if they are aware of their own Type, the inherent strengths, weaknesses, and interaction dynamics of their Type with clients' Type.

This awareness of their own Type is crucial to counselors, for with that awareness also comes more control over personal assumptions about what is "change", "growth", "good" counseling, and positive outcomes. I am often amused, for example, at the language of "change" and "growth". As an ENFP, when I use those words, I'm talking about self-actualization, awareness, self-support, and responsibility. An ST might be talking about concrete alterations in behavior, such as losing 10 pounds. The INT might be referring to some internal shift in thinking. With some of the 18 cases I would have set different counseling goals than the clients, if that were solely my domain. However, clients are the ones who must decide what they want to change, and what is important in their lives. Where a discrepancy in definition of change exists between counselor and client, counselors often may feel compelled to challenge clients' views. This challenge may be a valuable intervention in itself but may not necessarily result in complete client-counselor agreement about goals and desired change. To repeat a familiar axiom of the profession, counselors must start "where the client is".

I think counselors' awareness of these issues will lead them to be eclectic, that is to have several modalities they can use effectively with different Types of clients and problems. Although counselors may favor one therapeutic approach, which is probably a reflection of their own Type, they should have other counseling tools. Also, counselors aware of major differences with certain of their clients might consider using a consultant of dissimilar Type to themselves. This consultation could offer another perspective and enhance the counseling process. Of course, if counselor and client are very similar, a consultant of a different Type could also shed new light and energy on a therapeutic relationship that could get too comfortable or even stagnant. These are certainly issues for us to ponder as we work with clients.

The Value of the MBTI

I believe the 18 cases illustrate statements made in the first two chapters about the usefulness and specific applications of the MBTI. There is no need to reiterate all of those here. I do wish to underline the value of the conceptual framework of the Indicator for structuring interventions and establishing a common language between client and counselor. No matter what the specific use of the MBTI, it is consistently facilitative (when used appropriately) in identifying strengths and validating the individual. The 16 Types are 16 maps of developmental paths that can give counselors clues about where to look and how to proceed. I've found the MBTI particularly helpful in doing counseling outreach and prevention. Many of these cases wouldn't have come to me, or have come so soon, if that outreach had not occurred. Finally, knowledge of my own Type has heightened my awareness of the whole counseling process and helped me to monitor my own behavior, assumptions and expectations.

The Future

Many of us MBTI users have seen a dramatic increase in professional applications of the MBTI in the past few years, but we need more research in these applications. We hope the Indicator will be used in appropriate and ethical ways, and that clinicians will keep good data on Types, interventions, and so forth. Perhaps this casebook will stimulate other practitioners to submit cases from their counseling and consultation practices for possible publication in a second casebook. I invite response through the publisher to what I have written. There is a lot more to learn and discover!

- A list of publications—MBTI, Jungian, and other typology resources—can be obtained from CAPT, 2720 N.W. 6 St., Suite A, Gainesville, Florida, 32609, (904) 375-0160.

- CAPT maintains a comprehensive library, the Isabel Briggs Myers Memorial Library, with many dissertations that utilize the MBTI, as well as other materials.

- APT—the Association for Psychological Types—a professional organization with the purpose of educating, exchanging information, and assuring appropriate use of the MBTI. Same address as CAPT.

General References

Fordham, F. (1953). An introduction to Jung's psychology. New York: Penguin Books.

Gendlin, E. (1981). Focusing. Bantam.

Kiersey, D., & Bates, M. (1978). Please understand me. Del Mar, California: Promethean Books.

McCaulley, M. H. (1981). Jung's theory of psychological types and the Myers-Briggs Type Indicator. In P. McReynolds (Ed.), Advances in psychological assessment: Volume 5 (pp. 294-352). San Francisco: Jossey-Bass, Inc.

Myers, I. B. (1975). Manual: the Myers-Briggs Type Indicator. Palo Alto: Consulting Psychologists Press.

Myers, I. B. (1980). Gifts differing. Palo Alto: Consulting Psychologists Press.

Von Franz, M. L., & Hillman, J. (1979). Jung's typology. Irving, Texas: Spring Publications.

References: Type and Counseling

Bisbee, C., Mullaly, R., & Osmond, H. (1982). Type and psychiatric illness. Research in Psychological Type, 5, 49-68.

Carskadon, T. (1979). Clinical and counseling aspects of the Myers-Briggs Type Indicator: a research review. Research in Psychological Type, 2, 2-31.

Jones, J. H., & Sherman, R. (1979). Clinical uses of the Myers-Briggs Type Indicator. Research in Psychological Type, 2, 32-45.

Mendelsohn, G. (1966). Effects of client personality and client-counselor similarity on the duration of counseling: a replication and extension. Journal of Counseling Psychology, 13(2), 228-232.

Mendelsohn, G., & Geller, M. (1967). Similarity, missed sessions, and early termination. Journal of Counseling Psychology, 14(3), 210-215.

Thompson, C. (1977). The secondary school counselor's ideal client. Research in Psychological Type, 1, summer, 30-31.

References: Stability of Scores

Carlyn, M. (1977). An assessment of the Myers-Briggs Type Indicator. Journal of Personality Assessment, 41, 461-473.

Howes, R. J., & Carskadon, T. (1979). Test-retest reliabilities of the Myers-Briggs Type Indicator as a function of mood changes. Research in Psychological Type, 2, 67-72.

Stalcup, D. K. (1968). An investigation of personality characteristics of college students who do participate and those who do not participate in campus activities. Dissertation Abstracts International, 28, 4452A. (University Microfilms, No. 68-5897).

Myers, I. B. (1975). Manual: the Myers-Briggs Type Indicator. Palo Alto: Consulting Psychologists Press.